THINK ABOUT THESE THINGS

The Heavenly Mind

Tom Kingery

Author's Tranquility Press
MARIETTA, GEORGIA

Copyright © 2021 by Tom Kingery.

All rights reserved. No part of this publication may be reproduced, distributed or transmitted in any form or by any means, including photocopying, recording, or other electronic or mechanical methods, without the prior written permission of the publisher, except in the case of brief quotations embodied in critical reviews and certain other noncommercial uses permitted by copyright law. For permission requests, write to the publisher, addressed "Attention: Permissions Coordinator," at the address below.

Tom Kingery Author's Tranquility Press
2706 Station Club Drive SW
Marietta, GA 30060
www.authorstranquilitypress.com

Publisher's Note: This is a work of fiction. Names, characters, places, and incidents are a product of the author's imagination. Locales and public names are sometimes used for atmospheric purposes. Any resemblance to actual people, living or dead, or to businesses, companies, events, institutions, or locales is completely coincidental.

Ordering Information:
Quantity sales. Special discounts are available on quantity purchases by corporations, associations, and others. For details, contact the "Special Sales Department" at the address above.

Think About These Things/Tom Kingery
Paperback   ISBN: 978-1-957208-38-1
EBook   ISBN: 978-1-957208-39-8

Scripture quotations marked KJV are from the Holy Bible, King James Version (Authorized Version). First published in 1611. Quoted from the KJV Classic Reference Bible, Copyright © 1983 by The Zondervan Corporation.

Unless otherwise noted, scripture quotations are from the New Revised Standard Version Bible, Copyright© 1989 the Division of Christian Education of the National Council of the Churches of Christ in the United States of America. Used by permission. All rights reserved.

Scripture quotations marked ESV taken from The Holy Bible, English Standard Version ® (ESV®), Copyright© 2001 by Crossway, a publishing ministry of Good News Publishers. All rights reserved.

Scripture quotations marked HCSB are taken from the Holman Christian Standard Bible ®, Copyright© 1999, 2000, 2002, 2003, 2009 by Holman Bible Publishers.
Used by permission. Holman Christian Standard Bible®, Holman CSB®, and HCSB® are federally registered trademarks of Holman Bible Publishers.

Scripture quotations marked KJV are taken from the KingJames Version of the Bible.

Scripture quotations marked NASB are taken from The New American Standard Bible®, Copyright© 1960, 1962, 1963, 1968, 1971, 1972, 1973, 1975, 1977, 1995 by The Lockman Foundation. Used by permission.

Scripture quotations marked NIV are taken from The Holy Bible, New International Version®, NIV® Copyright © 1973, 1978, 1984, 2011 by Biblica, Inc.® Used by permission. All rights reserved worldwide.

Scripture quotations marked NKJV are taken from the New King James Version®.

Copyright© 1982 by Thomas Nelson. Used by permission. All rights reserved.

Contents

INTRODUCTION 7
Whatever is True 15
Whatever is Honorable 32
Whatever is Just 47
Whatever is Pure 71
Whatever is Pleasing 96
Whatever is Gracious 109
If there is any excellence 125
If there is anything worthy of Praise 140
Set your Mind on the Things of the Spirit 154
Conclusion 167
One Last Word 184

INTRODUCTION

How precious to me are your thoughts, Oh God! How vast is the sum of them!
PSALM 139:17 (NIV)

God has a mind. Created in God's likeness, we too have a mind. God has thoughts, and we do too. How wonderful to think about what God thinks. How awesome the depths. How glorious the heights. How perfect the perceptions.
Come, let us think.

The mind is related to the soul. We think with the mind. We believe with the mind. We remember with the mind. Though our souls may be the ultimate essence of our being, our eternal identity, the mind, the seat of our thoughts and feelings and will, determines who we are. I would not just say that "we are what we think," for we are much more than what we think, but I do want to claim that what we think certainly influences, to a great degree, who and what we are. The mind affects and influences our inner nature, our spiritual being, our heart, in such a way that Jesus could say that "if you are angry with a brother or sister, you will be liable to judgment" (Matthew 5:22). And He could say that "everyone who looks at a woman with lust has already committed adultery with her in his heart"(Matthew 5:28).

The central message, here, is that there is such a thing as sinful thoughts, and they are just as offensive to God as sinful actions. The mind affects the soul. Our state of mind affects the state of our soul.

The mind is not just a storage bank of memories. It is where the rubber hits the road. It is where those memories evoke feelings, and feelings evoke attitudes. It is where dreams become ideas and ideas become visions. It is where yearnings become hopes and hopes become joys. It is where desire becomes a hunger and that hunger creates passion and zeal. The mind is where the will discovers purpose and where faith becomes inspired. It is in the mind that we make decisions.

With our minds, we understand, we compare, we judge, we pray. It is where we believe and from where we communicate. In the mind, we meet our moods, our opinions, and our powers of reason. Our minds are where we meet the likeness of God within us from creation, for God too has a mind.

Because of all this, our minds are quite important. Our thoughts can be of great consequence. As much as negative thoughts can foster negative feelings, attitudes, and actions, so too can positive thoughts be a catalyst for positive feelings, attitudes, and actions. The power of positive thinking is nothing new. And the setting of faith provides much more than just positive thinking. It can evoke heavenly thoughts. In this context, I want to share a simple but sweeping embrace of a single passage of scripture from Paul's letter to the Christians of Philippi (4:8):

> Whatever is true,
> whatever is honorable,
> whatever is just,
> whatever is pure,
> whatever is pleasing,
> and whatever is gracious;
> if there is any excellence,
> if there is anything worthy of praise,
> think about these things.

I want to share what to me would be the heavenly mind.

In the chapters that follow, consider with me "these things" one by one, examining them, reviewing them, studying them, meditating on them. I call upon us all to apply our minds to what is true, to what is honorable, to what is just, to what is pure, to what is pleasing, to what is gracious. We are challenged to reflect on things of excellence and things worthy of praise. Let us realize that we are doing more than just entertaining ideas with our minds; we are contemplating things that can positively affect our eternal souls.

How important to you are your thoughts about God, about Christ, about the kingdom of heaven? What are the things you think about most? How do your thoughts affect you? How does what you think affect your behavior? How does what you think about others affect your attitudes toward them? I've already said that it's not entirely true that we are what we think, but I do believe that our relationships with God, with ourselves, with others, and with the world are based on our thoughts. As the proverb says, "As he thinks in his heart, so is he"(Proverbs 23:7 KJV).

***

Be transformed by the renewing of your mind.
ROMANS 12:2

Sometimes, the things we think about can renew us. There's the purpose of this book.

Faith is more than a heart thing. As important as it is to claim Christ in our hearts, we do it with our minds. Belief is an exercise of the mind; we have to think to believe. There may be a danger in intellectualizing the faith, but there is also a danger in depending only on our feelings, our hearts. "The heart is deceitful" (Jeremiah 17:9 NIV). But the mind can be deceitful, as well.

Let us never say that people who are developmentally delayed cannot have faith in Christ simply because their minds are unable to plumb the depths of truth or meditate theologically or think spiritually on issues of grace. Faith in Christ can be as simple as a child's trust and love. God has a special place in His heart for the "least" in this world. And we, who believe in Christ, are to bring Christ's love to them, but we have to care, and that takes some mental as well as emotional work.

So let's think. If we can reason, if we can deduce, if we can meditate, let us do so, for we can be convinced, we can be inspired, and we can be godly, for God created us to use these faculties, and so we should. Doing so can renew us, enlighten us, deepen us, and move us.

So think about what is true: trustworthy, real, constant, consistent, lasting, sound, valid, genuine, sincere, certain, legitimate, affirmative, faultless, perfect, unerring, honest.

Think about what is honorable: noble, reputable, commendable, worthy, respectable, upstanding, scrupulous, steadfast, ethical, high-principled, and decent.

Think about what is just: fair, right, righteous, equitable, legal, proper, correct, rational, and moral.

Think about what is pure: uncorrupt, unadulterated, untainted, unsoiled, undefiled, innocent, guilt-free, and sinless, beyond reproach.

Think about what is pleasing: lovely, delightful, beautiful, enjoyable, soothing, pleasant, agreeable, charming, appealing, adorable, and splendid.

Think about what is gracious: kind, benevolent, commendable, honorable, tender, considerate, nice, merciful, congenial, thoughtful, and compassionate.

Think about what is excellent: perfect, superb, valuable, meritorious, of good quality, above par, high caliber, virtuous, magnificent, wonderful, glorious, the best.

Think about what is praiseworthy: laudable, worthy of compliment, pleasing, better than expected, blessed, admirable, well deserving.

Think about these things. The lists could probably go on far longer than what has been mentioned just now. Surely, they have not been exhausted. But this is a beginning. Dwell on these things, and you can renew your mind. Let these things be food for your soul. Remember what is virtuous and inspiring, what you have experienced, what you have seen in others and in the world around you. Make them a large part of your conversations. Begin to live in this world with a heavenly mind. Though doing so may not change the world, it will change you, renew you, and you can change the world, for thoughts can be the catalyst for actions.

It's also relevant to consider what not to think. Now, I know from experience that as soon as we are told what not to think, that's all we can focus on. I had a philosophy professor in college who taught this lesson. He wrote the word "rhinoceros" on the chalkboard and said, "Whenever you hear the word existentialism, do not think of the word rhinoceros!" It's funny, because, to this day, over forty years later, every time I hear the word existentialism or existential, the word rhinoceros flashes before my mind. Maybe, however, if I give us a whole list of words telling us what not to think, it will be different. The intention, however, is that mentioning the opposites or the contrary to what we should think will bring into focus the very things we are supposed to think. I've done this when I taught the Ten Commandments; stating the opposites of each commandment helps bring the particular law into focus a bit more clearly. For example, being commanded to have no other gods before God: Be loyal to the one God. Being commanded to honor your father and mother: do not dishonor them. If "Thou shall not kill" is the commandment, bring more life to the situation. And so on. Try it; it is a good spiritual exercise and helps us understand how we think about things.

So as you think about whatever is true, do not think about what is false, fraudulent, deceitful, lies, gossip, pretentious, hypocritical, exaggerative, and diminishing of what is real, or lacking integrity.

As you think about whatever is honorable, do not think about what is dishonorable, disrespectful, crooked, treacherous, improper, or inexcusable.

As you think about whatever is just, do not think about what is unjust, unfair, wrong, oppressive, inequitable, unsportsmanlike, or sinful.

As you think about whatever is pure, do not think about what is impure, corrupt, unclean, dirty, defiling, contaminating, or compromising.

As you think about whatever is pleasing, do not think about what is displeasing, unenjoyable, distasteful, disagreeable, undesirable, offensive, abominable, or uninspiring.

As you think about whatever is gracious, do not think about what is disgraceful, shameful, embarrassing, disrespectful, humiliating, scandalous, or unkind.

As you think about whatever is excellent, do not think about what is inferior, mediocre, shabby, poorly done, deficient, base, unimportant, or unimpressive.

As you think about whatever is worthy of praise, do not think about what is condemnable, blameworthy, unfavorable, disgusting, reproachful, disappointing, or indifferent.

Note, however, that as we focus on the things that make up the heavenly mind, the absence of them in our surroundings will be more noticed. For example, the more we focus on what is just, the more we may be aware of injustices in the world. The more we focus on what is pure, the more we may recognize what is corrupt.

The goal is to focus, to zero in on what God wants us to think about. The more we turn to godly thoughts, the more we will experience the renewing of our minds. The more we meditate on what is divine, the more we will think godly things.

Let's begin with prayer.

A Prayer

0 Lord, You are unchanging, but You change us. You call us to be transformed by the renewing of our minds. Help us, then, to set our minds on things that are above and not on things that are on earth. But let our thoughts turn to actions that bring Your Kingdom into our midst. Fill our hearts with love. Change us from within, and we shall be true. This we ask in the name of Jesus Christ, our Lord. Amen.

CHAPTER ONE

Whatever is True

> To set the mind on the flesh is death, but to set the mind on the Spirit is life and peace.
> ROMANS 8:6 (ESV)

There are two sides to the truth: the facts and what they mean. People often believe that to know the facts is to possess their meaning. But it seems to be a rare thing when the meaning is truly manifested in the heart. In Paul's letter to the Ephesians, he says, "Speaking the truth in love, we must grow up in every way into Him who is the head, into Christ" (4:15). The meaning of the eternal facts in our lives reveals a mature and more complete faith. Remember that faith without love is nothing (1 Corinthians 13:2). We may know what is true, but we may not go all the way into the truth. Or I should say, the truth does not come all the way into us. We often cling to some false images of what we think is true, and we reject the challenges to our own ways of thinking. We justify ourselves rather than God.

> You are those who justify yourselves in the sight of others; but God knows your hearts; for what is prized by human beings is an abomination in the sight of God. (Luke 16: 15)

In his letter to the Romans, Paul tells us, "Do not be conformed to this world, but be transformed by the renewing of your mind, that you may discern what is the will of God, what is good and acceptable and perfect" (12:2). He means there are worldly principles to which people who live in the world tend to conform. But since a Christian is meant to be in the world but not of the world, we are called upon to live by principles, by a mind-set, and by a point of view that proves a greater and truer way. "I am about to create new heavens and a new earth; the former things shall not be remembered or come to mind" (Isaiah 65:17).

Do not think about former things. Paul calls us to think about other things, better things.

> Whatever is true,
> whatever is honorable,
> whatever is just,
> whatever is pure,
> whatever is *pleasing,*
> whatever is gracious,
> if there is any excellence,
> if there is anything worthy of praise,
> think about these things.
> (Philippians 4:8; emphasis mine)

So let's consider whatever is true. By doing so, we can begin to know what is true and discover how "the truth will make you free" (John 8:32).

Start with Jesus Christ, who proclaimed that He Himself is "the way, the truth, and the life" (John 14:6; emphasis mine).

And He said, "If you continue in My Word [the Word of Truth], you are truly My disciples, and you will know the truth and the truth will make you free" (John 8:31-32).

To understand something more about what all this means, look at the dialogue in the Gospel of John between Jesus and Pilate. The question on the table becomes, "Are You the King of the Jews?" Jesus gives a somewhat cryptic answer. He says, "My Kingdom is not of this world." To this, Pilate says, "So you *are* a king?" Then Jesus answers, "You say that I am a king. For this I was born and for this I came into the world: to testify to the truth. Everyone who belongs to the truth listens to My voice." And finally, Pilate just says, "What is truth?" (John 18:33-38; emphasis mine).

I believe that Christ's kingdom is a kingdom of truth. It is a kingdom of nothing but truth. The kingdom Jesus reveals, the kingdom to which Jesus gives witness, the kingdom that is freedom from sin, is also a kingdom of love. It is a kingdom in which we are called to walk in fellowship with one another. It's a kingdom where "if we say we have fellowship with Him while we [actually] walk in darkness, we lie, and do not do what is true" (1John 1:6).

Jesus also promised to send the Holy Spirit, a holy comforter who would be a counselor and the Spirit of Truth, "whom the world cannot receive, because it neither sees Him nor knows Him. You know Him, for He abides with you, and will be in you"(John 14:17).

To live according to the truth is to live honestly and with sincerity. It is to be genuine and real. In a world where living a lie is all too common, to live according to the truth is to stand upon lasting principles.

Think about these things: the principle of trust and not deceit, the principle of authenticity rather than artificiality, the principle of lasting goodness and not faulty inadequacy, and the principle of encouragement rather than critical negativity.

Think about these things: Whatever is true is real, complete, and consistent. Whatever is true is sound; it has integrity and is unpretentious. Think about these things: They are virtuous qualities we should desire for ourselves. They are characteristics we should seek. Do we? Do we seek these characteristics intentionally?

"Run to and fro through the streets of Jerusalem! Look and take note! Search her squares to see if you can find one person who acts justly and seeks the truth" (Jeremiah 5:1). If God sent someone into our midst looking for just one person who really sought the truth, who would he or she find? Who could you name? If you seek the truth, are you easy to find? Has it become old-fashioned to consider braving a quest for truth? Or do we conform to the world by associating with people who are false? How many people can you really trust? Are they authentic? Does the Spirit of Truth, the Spirit of Christ, dwell in them?

What is the relationship between truth and faith, between trust and belief, and between reality and integrity? Think about these things.

> Examine yourselves to see whether you are living in the faith.
>
> Test yourselves. Do you not realize that Jesus Christ is in you?-Unless indeed you fail to meet the test! I hope you will find out that we have not failed. But we pray God that you may do nothing wrong-not that we may appear to have met the test, but that you may do what is right, though we may seem to have failed. For *we cannot do anything against the truth, but only for the truth*
>
> (2 Corinthians 13:5-8; emphasis mine)

Every teacher, pastor, and other leader should be willing to say such things. Even our falseness, by its negative example, reveals the truth when it is discerned as flawed and seen as hypocrisy.

How does *your* life reveal the truth? Is your example that of someone who has "fastened the belt of truth around your waist" (Ephesians 6:14)? Realize that today we dress ourselves with a belt. Our belts hold up our pants. Is your example that of someone who has on a belt of truth? Or do you find yourself embarrassed, as if your pants fell down because you did not have the proper belt to hold up what you should uphold?

Set your mind upon the truth, honesty, sincerity, and integrity. Think about these things. Consider what is genuine. Fix your vision on goals more virtuous, including developing a character more true to what you believe in your heart. Realize that "a doubleminded man is unstable" (James 1:8 KJV). Rise to the call to be true, and you will reach new heights. Your mind will be transformed. Seek not only authenticity, but battle against artificiality. Seek not only to find truth but also to conquer deceit. Walk in the light, as Jesus is in the light, and we will have true fellowship with one another, and the acceptance we will feel will make it seem like the blood of Jesus has truly cleansed us from all sin (1John 1:7). For the fellowship of the kingdom of truth, the kingdom of faith, is one where falseness is not known but brought to the light. It is where blessings are affirmed and where the Christ in others, the spirit of truth, is made real.

When we think about one another, let us not dwell on the negative. Accentuate the positive. Have higher hopes for others- and for yourself- and the meaning of your lives will take on a whole new depth. Your own faith will become deeper because of it. See beyond just the facts. Capture the meaning behind them. See beyond just what another person says or does, and try to fathom the reason their lives evoke the words and actions you experience.

And think about this: We are those who walk not according to the flesh, but according to the Spirit [the spirit of eternal truth]. For those who live according to the flesh set their minds on the things of the flesh, but those who live according to the Spirit set their minds on the things of the Spirit. To set the mind on the flesh is death, but to set the mind on the Spirit is life and peace. (Romans 8:4-6)

What does it mean to walk according to the Spirit but to continue in the Word of Jesus Christ?

If you continue in My Word, you are truly my disciples; and you will know the truth, and the truth will make you free. (John 8:31-32)

To inspire you to think about whatever is true, study what is in the scriptures.

"The Word became flesh and lived among us. We have seen his glory, the glory as of a father's only Son, full of grace and truth" (John 1:14).

"When the Advocate comes, whom I will send to you from the Father - the Spirit of truth who comes from the Father-he will testify on My behalf" (John 15:26).

"Lead me in your truth and teach me, for you are God of my salvation, for You I wait all day long" (Psalm 25:5).

"Keep your tongue from evil and your lips from speaking deceit" (Psalm 34:13).

"He gave us birth by the word of truth, that we would become a kind of first-fruits of His creatures" (James 1:18).

"Above all, my beloved, do not swear-neither by heaven or by earth or by any other oath. But let your 'Yes' be yes, and your 'No' be no, so that you may not fall under condemnation" (James 5:12).

"Again, you have heard that it was said to those of ancient times, 'You shall not swear falsely, but carry out the vows you have made to the Lord.' But I say to you, do not swear at all: either by heaven, for it is God's throne; or by the earth, for it is his footstool; or by Jerusalem, for it is the city of the Great King. And do not swear by your head, for you cannot make one hair white or black. Let your word be 'Yes, Yes' or 'No,

No'; anything else comes from the evil one"(Matthew 5:33-37).

"Little children, let us love, not in word or speech but in truth and action" (1 John 3:18).

"We know that the Son of God has come and has given us understanding, so that we may know him who is true. And we are in him who is true, in his Son Jesus Christ. He is the true God and eternal life"(1Joh n 5:20).

"I have no greater joy than to hear that my children are walking in the truth" (3John 1:4).

"God is spirit, and those who worship Him must worship in the Spirit and in truth" (Joh n 4:24).

"Do your best to present yourself to God as one approved by Him, a worker who has no need to be ashamed, rightly explaining the word of truth" (2 Timothy 2:15).

Stories

A very wealthy man had a trusted steward who watched over and cared for his sprawling estate. After many years, the landowner summoned the steward and asked him to build a new house on a beautiful lot in a corner of the estate. "Spare no expense. I want this house to be perfect," he told his steward. The man went to work arranging the construction, and the project began. Over the weeks, however, he began to let resentment worm its way into his thoughts: *Why should my master have so much while I continue to live so humbly?*

He began to cut corners. He was the only one to know about the inferior quality of some of the hidden things in the construction process. It would still be a wonderful house, but it wouldn't really be perfect.

Well, when everything was complete, he called the master to inspect the home. "Beautiful! Perfect. You have done better than I imagined," said the master.
But the steward felt shrewd; no one would ever know that the house wasn't as great as it appeared.

The next day, the master summoned the steward. Holding a large envelope in his hand, he said, "I wanted you to know how much I have appreciated all you have done for me, and I want to reward you for all your years in my service."

And he handed him the keys to the house and the title, telling him he could retire now and that a trust had been established, providing him with a wonderful income for the rest of his life.

The steward's eyes welled up with tears ... but the master never knew that they were not just tears of joy and appreciation, but also tears of sorrow over his own foolishness.
The truth hurt him. He hurt himself. Sometimes, the truth comes as a surprise. Sometimes, it exposes us to ourselves.

One evening, a woman who loved to gossip noticed that for several hours, a certain car was parked on the street outside her neighbor's house, a few doors down. Later, she found out that the car belonged to the Methodist minister. She let the gossip fly, imagining an affair while her husband was nowhere to be seen. The truth was that her husband had been through some very serious medical tests, and the pastor was simply showing care for the man and his wife. When the source of the gossip was discovered, the minister visited the woman who started it all. Of course, she denied everything. The pastor apologized for thinking she had anything to do with the falseness of the gossip. When he left, he walked home, leaving his car outside her house ... overnight. The truth has a way of making itself known, and gossip is just plain wrong, especially when our ideas become exaggerated in our minds.

A young girl spent half an hour in her needlework class, embroidering a beautiful flower. When the teacher came around to inspect her handiwork, she was sure she would admire the way things were looking. Instead, the teacher turned the fabric over and shook her head. In her effort to make an impressive flower on the side she knew would show, she had paid no attention to the back of the fabric on which she worked-the hidden part. Her teacher pointed out some clumsy knots, the untidy way she had fastened off some threads, and even a few loose ends. It was not just a little upsetting for the young girl to have to completely undo her flower and embroider it again.

She learned a valuable lesson that day. She realized how often she had tried to make a good impression by only offering a good outward appearance. Even though everything may look good on the surface, God sees the hidden parts and is not deceived. Integrity.

A man was accused of murder. He didn't do it. He was framed, and his lawyer believed him. When another man was put on the witness stand, the lawyer scrutinized his alibi, found several inconsistencies, and exposed the truth before the court and the jury. Fin ally, in exasperation, the true murderer confessed the crime, and the accused man was literally set free by the truth.

John 8:3- 11 discusses the woman caught in the act of adultery:

The scribes and the Pharisees brought a woman who had been caught in adultery, and making her stand before all of them, they said to him, "Teacher, this woman has been caught in the very act of adultery. Now, in the Law, Moses commanded us to stone such women. Now what do you say?" This they said to test him, so that they might have some charge to bring against him. Jesus bent down and wrote with his finger on the ground. When they kept questioning Him, he straightened up and said to them, "Let anyone among you who is without sin be the first to throw a stone at her." And once again he bent down and wrote on the ground. When they heard it, they went away, one by one, beginning with the elders, and Jesus was left alone with the woman standing before Him. Jesus straightened up and said to her, "Woman, where are they? Has no one condemned you?" She said, "No one, Sir." And Jesus said, "Neither do I condemn you; go your way, and from now on do not sin again."

The truth, again, set someone free. This time, the freedom came as the truth about all the woman's accusers was exposed. No one is entirely guiltless, and therefore, no one is qualified to be so judgmental. The truth is very liberating, and God's forgiveness can truly set us free. But never forget how the woman was told to sin no more.

Acts 5:1-5 says, "A man named Ananias, with the consent of his wife Sapphira, also sold a piece of property. With his wife's knowledge he kept back some of the proceeds, and brought only a part and laid it at the apostles' feet. 'Ananias,' Peter asked, 'Why has Satan filled your heart to lie to the Holy Spirit and to keep back part of the proceeds for the land?

While it remained unsold, did it not remain your own? And after it was sold, were not the proceeds at your disposal? How is it that you have contrived this deed in your heart? You did not lie to us but to God.' Now when Ananias heard these words, he fell down and died. And great fear seized all who heard it."

What to Do

Be honest. Do not assume that because you know the facts, you understand their meaning. A musician might know the music and then just play the notes without any feeling. An artist might carve a statue perfectly, but it may only look like a statue. Don't overestimate your knowledge, nor your understanding. Admit your limitations. Tell the truth. Let anything you say add to life a greater depth, a better light. Let no darkness occur because of you. Sir Walter Scott said in his poem, *Marmion*, that it's a tangled web we weave, when we practice to deceive. The thread of one lie leads to the necessity of making another lie, and, so on, until it is so complicated that it entangles you. Don't lie. You shall not bear false witness (Exodus 20:16). It's one of the Ten Commandments.

Examine yourself. When have you justified your own ways, even though the word of truth tells you it was wrong: "I lied to protect my friends," "I did what I did because it was the lesser of two evils," "I acted that way because I wanted the promotion," "That's okay for you, but not for me," "Live and let live," "You go your way; I'll go mine," "Do your own thing," "If it feels good, do it" (the pleasure principle: horrible lie), "It's not wrong if it doesn't hurt anyone." Do not justify yourself, justify God.

Do not be pretentious. I have known people who will say that everything is fine, but beneath the surface, their lives are in disarray: a relationship is broken, a job may have unnecessary tensions, or some fears within may be paralyzing them. Some people like to think of themselves as better than others, look down on others, or give them the cold shoulder. The truth is, "there is no one who is righteous, not even one; there is no one who has understanding; there is no one who seeks God. All have turned aside, together they have become worthless; there is no one who shows kindness, there is not even one"(Romans 3:10- 12).

Don't exaggerate. I have often experienced how people make mountains out of molehills or blow things out of proportion. A little offense, when rehearsed in the mind, can become a horrible grievance. Don't let that happen.

Don't water down the truth. Many people will reduce the Christian faith to John 3:16: "God so loved the world that He gave His only Son, so that everyone who believes in Him may not perish but may have eternal life." It is watered down to just a matter of belief. And for too many, belief is simply intellectual ascent, so faith is intellectualized, and little is taken to heart. Dietrich Bonhoeffer taught us something about what is called cheap grace: "the preaching of forgiveness without requiring repentance, baptism without church discipline. Communion without confession. Cheap grace is grace without discipleship, grace without the cross, and grace without Jesus Christ." This is taught in his excellent book The Cost of Discipleship. When we water down the truth, we are cheapening the cost. I believe this could include the idea of discipleship without worship; giving without sacrifice; expecting heaven without holiness; righteousness without obedience, and so on. Truth. On the cross, Jesus cried out, "Father, forgive them, for they do not know what they are doing" (Luke 23:34). "If only they knew," we might say. If only they knew the truth. There is too much ignorance in this world: people ignoring the truth, and people indifferent to the truth. The truth gives light. We need to seek it, share it, and fight against the darkness.

Confess your falseness. If we say we have fellowship with Him while we are in darkness, we lie and do not do what is true. But if we walk in the light as He Himself is in the light, we have fellowship with one another, and the blood of Jesus His Son cleanses us from all sin" (1 John 1:6-7).

Study the truth. Read the truth as published in philosophy books. Check statistics in order to know what some of the facts are. Just be careful; I knew a man who often said, "75 percent of statistics are just made up to prove your own argument." (Again, don't lie.) Attend a Bible study, a class at church, or a workshop/seminar/forum. Grow deeper in your understanding. It may be wonderful to read the Bible on your own, but it's better to discuss God's Word with others. Pay extra attention to the sermon during worship; what are you learning?

Defend the truth. Christian apologists are needed these days more than ever. Many false ideas continue to capture the fancy of people who are only half-hearted believers. People still fall prey to worldliness, greed, acquisitiveness, and indifference, and they neglect the needs of others. The Christian faith is often overlooked or mocked by the worldly. Stand up for what you believe, especially when God's name is taken in vain or offensive language is used in your midst. You need to stand up for what is righteous. And you need to compel people out of their indifference. Indifference has infiltrated the ranks even while you battle against it.

Teach the truth. If there is a shortage of church school teachers in your congregation, volunteer. Don't wait to be an expert; every curriculum has teaching aids. Open your door for Bible study, book study (lots of Christian books come with study questions), social interaction, and faithful fellowship. Invite someone else to lead until you feel comfortable doing so. The possibilities are extensive.

Prove that you can be trusted. Do not gossip. Be loyal to friends; to church; to God. Can people count on you? Do you trust others?

A Prayer
O almighty God, in Jesus Christ, You revealed the truth; when we receive the Holy Spirit, we receive the spirit of truth. Give us grace to know the blessings of Your way and the true life that can be known through Your Word, and help us to understand what is real and unchanging, what is absolute and irreducible, and what is unable to be denied. In our hearts,

help us to be honest and full of integrity, resisting all false pretense and deceitful thoughts until we are known for Your influence in our lives. This we pray in Jesus's name. Amen.

A Song
Envision a kingdom of nothing but truth,
where love is the promise to old age and youth.
From the babe to the dying, from the strong to the lame, envision a King who can call you by name.

Envision a kingdom where blessings abound,
where you will be welcomed, and you will be crowned.
And you'll be forgiven, and you will be free.
Envision a lifetime of eternity.

We can learn how to follow where justice may lead.
We can learn how to feel it when someone else bleeds.
We can learn to forgive; we can learn we are frail.
We can learn to accept when another may fail.

We can know a compassion that conquers our fears. We can witness the comfort that wipes away tears.
We'll be part of a Spirit, a power to live.
And though we have nothing, there's love we can give.

Envision this kingdom over all of the earth. The kingdom's for us from the moment of birth. Envision the kingdom; today is the day.
Just come follow Jesus, for He is the way.

I believe in this wonderful kingdom I share.
I believe there's a day when we all will be there.
I believe we can make it if we all follow through.
I believe we can make it if you believe too.

CHAPTER TWO

Whatever is Honorable

> When one is honored, all rejoice.
> 1 CORINTHIANS 12:26B

Consider for a moment what, to the world, the greatest honors seem to be. There are crowns for beauty; there are trophies, rings, and awards for competitive team victories. There are medals for superior athletic abilities. There are medals for bravery in battle, intellectual achievements, and civic benevolence. Perhaps one of the greatest honors is to receive a Nobel Prize. Awards are given for a multitude of reasons: talent, intelligence, courage, invention, discovery, and even popularity. Public notoriety is given to Hollywood stars, even though their fame is partly due to popularity or scandal. How many Hollywood stars have been dishonored by scandals? Of **all** of these things, some are worthy of honor, but are they all really honorable?

The apostle Paul said that we should show honor where honor is due (Romans 13:7). But he also gave an example of the way we tend to consider the wrong things to be honorable. He was concerned with the outward show that makes people feel confident that they have some special status in life. He said, "If anyone else has reason to be confident in the flesh, I have more: circumcised on the eighth day, a member of the people of Israel, of the tribe of Benjamin, a Hebrew born of Hebrews; as to the Law, a Pharisee; as to zeal, a persecutor of the Church; as to righteousness under the Law, blameless" (Philippians 3:4-6).

Too often, we confuse honor with pride. The things we are proud of are not always things that are truly honorable, especially from the point of view of faith, the heavenly mind. We imagine that the things we are proud of are things that are honorable, and sometimes they are. But look at what Paul says next: "Yet whatever gain I had, these I have come to regard as loss because of Christ. More than that, I regard everything as loss because of the surpassing value of knowing Christ Jesus my Lord. For His sake, I have suffered the loss of all things, and I regard them as rubbish [the King James Version says "dung"], in order that I may gain Christ, and be found in Him, not having a righteousness of my own ... but one that comes through faith in Christ" (Philippians 3:7-9).

What is commendable about you? Is it your righteousness before the law? Is it your status, your income, your heritage, your past? Do you rest on past laurels and say that you've done a good thing; been there, done that, you don't need to do anymore? If the most commendable thing to the most honorable apostle is knowing Christ, where do you fit in? And what actions or deeds do you commend others for doing? What does our culture deem commendable?

In a culture where beauty and youth are honored with crowns and admiration; in an era where great fame is bestowed to immoral and unscrupulous men and women; when we are bombarded by slogans that project an image of cool upon things as superficial as jeans and shoes, or an image of sexy is bottled in perfume and cologne, what are we saying to ourselves about the true virtues? We never even seem to think about them. They are not publicized or advertised. Is it really virtuous to have a certain car? Is it really virtuous to be promiscuous and to have made so many sexual conquests? Is it virtuous to be capable of drinking large amounts of alcohol? Is it virtuous to be a party animal? Or to be a fox? Or a hunk? Ask the college coed, frat boy, or sorority sister. Or is all that, as Paul would say, rubbish compared to knowing Jesus Christ?

Consider, though, the things we apparently think are honorable, particularly the things that are reflected back to us through the media. And use the following questions to test their honorability: First of all, is it the truth? Does it have some falseness or pretense to it? Does it have a lasting legitimacy, or is it superficial in some way? Is it artificial? Will it be commendable to you tomorrow? When you're older? If you were younger? Does what you consider worthy of honor reflect a sense of decency? Is it respectable? Would it be honorable to everyone? Your parents? Your children? Or is it only honorable now, to your group of peers? Is it constructive? Does it build good will and better relationships?

I admire the Rotary test for all the things that they think, say, or do; the test has four points: 1) Is sit the truth? 2) Is it fair to all concerned? 3) Will it build good will and better friendships? 4) Will it be beneficial to all concerned? Other organizations may also have standards for ethical behavior, but the point to be made is that we need standards.

Test an action or a thought by whether or not it is respectable, proper, or decent. If it is not, it is not honorable. Some translations of this passage of scripture use the word *noble* instead of *honorable*. Think about the nobility of someone's actions. Do they reflect a higher moral principle, a standard to which people might aspire? If yes, this is what it means to be honorable.

Another way to test the things you might cheer on or commend is simply to question what you might think would be the opinion of others. As far as your actions are concerned, would you feel comfortable including your parents, teachers, pastor, or priest in what you do? What would they think? What would God think? Would it honor Jesus Christ? A good test that has been popularized among Christians of the current generation is the phrase "What Would Jesus Do?" WWJD?

Think about what you might wear. Would you feel comfortable wearing it if Jesus was present? Would you wear it to church for worship?

Do your values and morals conflict with your faith? Are they worldly and materialistic, or are they spiritual and inspirational? Remember, now, "to set the mind on things of the flesh is death" (Romans 8:6). What principles govern your behavior?

How about the use of your money, time, talents, energy; how could they be better used to make you more honorable?

Never confuse wealth with honorability. Even though our culture seems to commend people who achieve prominence in the world of finance, not every rich person is truly honorable. Likewise with fame. Just because someone has acquired fame, they are not automatically honorable. Talented people often seek the spotlight simply because it feels good to be admired for what they can do. Check the motivation that compels someone to be so popular. Some do it as pleasure seekers. Think of some rock stars or movie stars. Their lifestyle may look pleasurable from a worldly point of view, but are they really honorable? In Luke 16:15, Jesus said, "What is prized by human beings is an abomination in the sight of God." We may not realize it, but the things that inflate our egos are often detestable in God's eyes. The ego is a funny thing, though. Human beings need esteem, encouragement, and appreciation. We are called on by Paul to build one another up (1 Thessalonians 5:11). But the context has to do with our hope in the final triumph of Christ. In the fourth chapter of this Epistle, we are instructed "to live and to please God" (4:1). Likewise, lead a life worthy of the calling to which you have been called (Ephesians 4:1).

And your thoughts: are they honorable? If your thoughts could be projected in front of everybody, or if everyone could read your mind, would your thoughts be honorable? Or would you sometimes be ashamed of them? I know I am. At times, I have wished, in envy, to have other circumstances surrounding me: more wealth, more luxury, more pleasure, but I have spiritual checks and balances that bring me back to my purpose as a person of faith: to glorify God in all I think, say, and do. I am embarrassed by the moments when I have been frustrated enough to swear or painful enough to want to escape. Seldom would I want others to know how I was feeling at the time. But I need to remember, always, that what I think can affect my soul.

In the story of Esther, Haman was disappointed by his thoughts (Esther 6:1-12; read the story below). Haman hated Mordecai. He wanted him hanged, but the king ordered him to honor the man. Haman thought he was big stuff, but Mordecai had been the real hero. Haman's thoughts left him twisting in the wind.

Jesus calls upon His disciples not to honor themselves, or to suppose themselves to be honorable, but to be humble. See the story of the guests at the wedding feast below. Why do we fail to humble ourselves, especially knowing that the humble will be exalted, from heaven's point of view?

In the Gospel of John, Jesus said, "Whoever serves Me, the Father will honor them" (12:26). He also said, "Anyone who does not honor the Son does not honor the Father"(John 5:23). What are you doing to honor the one who is truly honorable? Of course, God is not only honorable; God is glorious! We should glorify God.

What is honorable to you? In the book of Hebrews, we are taught that "Jesus is worthy of more glory than Moses as the builder of a house has more honor than the house. For every house is built by someone ... and we are His house" (3:3-4, 6).

The apostle Peter instructed the faithful to "honor everyone" (1 Peter 2:17) at a minimum, I would say, do not dishonor anyone. Offend no one. Do not do anything that would make others ashamed to know you. Do things, think things that will evoke a sense of blessing in others, a sense of honorability in the knowledge that you are one of us. And we will be glad because your deeds are worthy of respect and acknowledgment in such a way that we can feel pride and honored by your honorability.

Think about things that are honorable. The more you think about them, the more you will do them.

To inspire you to think about whatever is honorable, study what is in the scriptures:

"Humility goes before honor"(Proverbs 18:12 NIV).

"Then I heard every creature in heaven and on the earth and under the earth and in the sea, and all that is in them, singing, 'To the One seated on the throne, and to the Lamb, be blessing and honor and glory and might forever and ever'" (Revelation 5:13).

"Honor the Lord with your substance and with the first of all your produce" (Proverbs 3:9).

"Pray for us. We are sure that we have a clear conscience desiring to act honorably in all things" (Hebrews 13:18).

"A good name is better than precious ointment" (Ecclesiastes 7:1).

"A good name is to be chosen rather than great riches. And favor is better than silver or gold" (Proverbs 22:1).

"So a bishop must be above reproach" (1 Timothy 3:2-7).

"Let no one despise your youth; but set the believers an example in speech and conduct, in conversation, in love, in faith, in purity" (1 Timothy 4:12).

"Let your light so shine before others, so that they may see your good works, and give glory to your Father in heaven" (Matthew 5:16).

"Conduct yourselves honorably among the Gentiles, so that, though they malign you as evildoers, they may see your honorable deeds, and glorify God when he comes to judge" (1 Peter 2:12).

"But even if you do suffer for doing what is right, you are blessed. Do not fear what they fear, and do not be intimidated, but in your hearts sanctify Christ as Lord. Always be ready to make your defense to anyone who demands from you an accounting for the hope that is in you, yet do it with gentleness and reverence. Keep your conscience clear, so that, when you are maligned, those who abuse you for your good conduct in Christ may be put to shame" (1 Peter 3:14-16).

"Dead flies make the perfumer's ointment give off a foul odor, so a little folly outweighs wisdom and honor" (Ecclesiastes 10:1).

"Likewise, urge the younger men to be self-controlled. Show yourself in all respects a model of good works, and in your teaching show integrity, gravity, and sound speech that cannot be censured; then any opponent will be put to shame, having nothing evil to say of us" (Titus 2:6- 8).

Stories

"On that night, the king could not sleep, and he commanded to bring the book of records, the annals; and they were read to the king. And it was found written how Mordecai had told of Bigthana and Teresh, two of the king's eunuchs, who guarded the threshold, and who had conspired to assassinate King Ahasuerus. Then the king said, 'What honor or distinction has been bestowed on Mordecai for this?' The king's servants who attended him said, 'Nothing has been done for him.'

"The king said, 'Who is in the court?' Now Haman had just entered the outward court of the king's palace, to speak unto the king about having Mordecai hanged on the gallows that he had prepared for him. So the king's servants said unto him, 'Haman is there, standing in the court.' The king said, 'Let him come in.' So Haman came in. And the king said unto him, 'What shall be done for the man whom the king wishes to honor?'

"Haman said to himself, 'Whom would the king wish to honor more than me?' So Haman said to the king, 'For the man whom the king wishes to honor, let royal robes be brought, which the king has worn, and the horse that the king has ridden, with a royal crown on his head. Let this robe and the horse be handed over to one of the king's most noble officials; let him robe the man whom the king wishes to honor, and let him conduct the man on horseback through the open square of the city, proclaiming before him: "Thus shall it be done for the man whom the king wishes to honor." Then the king said to Haman, 'Quickly, take the robes and the horse, as you have said.' So Haman took the robes and the horse, and robed

Mordecai, and led him riding through the open square of the city, proclaiming, 'Thus shall it be done unto the man whom the king wishes to honor.' Then Mordecai returned to the king's gate. But Haman hurried to his house mourning, and with his head covered" (Esther 6:1- 12 KJV).

"When he noticed how the guests chose the places of honor, he told them a parable: 'When you are invited by someone to a wedding banquet, do not sit down at the place of honor, in case someone more distinguished than you has been invited by your host; and the host who invited both of you may come and say to you, "Give this person your place." And then, in disgrace, you would start to take the lowest place. But when you are invited, go and sit down at the lowest place, so that when your host comes, he may say to you, "Friend, move up higher." Then you will be honored in the presence of all who sit at the table with you. For all who exalt themselves will be humbled, and those who humble themselves will be exalted"' (Luke 14:7- 11).

In the movie *While You Were Sleeping*, Peter Gallagher plays a man who fell at an elevated train station and was badly injured. Sandra Bullock rescues him, and while he was in a coma, she came to the hospital to see if he was all right. She had pretended to be his fiancée in order to get in to see him. He doesn't recognize her, and everyone presumes he has some degree of amnesia. His family takes her in because they think she really is his fiancée. There is a moment in the movie, after he becomes conscious again, where they have a conversation about heroism. She felt like he was a hero every day for giving up his seat on the train for someone else. That's not really heroic, he says. She tells him, "It is to the one who gets to sit down." As a boy, he rescued three baby squirrels who had fallen from a tree. Later, in a moment of awakening, he confesses to his brother that he had actually knocked them out of the tree with a rock, and then, guilt-ridden, he "rescued" the little critters. He had humbly allowed himself to be honored for his heroic deed. In a way, the movie is about honor and honorability, whether it is deserved or not. But the scene where he confesses to his brother is very revealing. He knew he didn't deserve to be honored, but he accepted it. Honor where honor is due.

A cruel father insisted that his young son honor him. Scripture demanded it in the Fifth Commandment. The boy was confused, but he still said and did things that showed respect and love for the man. As the boy grew older and was able to discern the truth of his circumstances, he was unwilling to endure the beatings and verbal abuse of his father. He became aware of how the cruelty of his father came from alcohol- infused tirades. His father was a drunk, taking out his frustrations on the boy and his mother. One day, after another alcoholic rage, the boy lashed back, partly protecting his mother and partly in rebellion. "You want me to honor you," he says, "but you are not honorable. I am commanded to honor you because you are my father. Here's what I will do. I will *not* honor you. No longer will I say or do anything that commends you in any way unless you truly deserve it. But ... because you are my father and I am your son, I will, at the least, live so as never to dishonor you."

The father changed his ways. The boy grew to be a very successful businessman, such that the father could be proud, and he felt honored. The change in the father led him to church and penitential remorse. Over the years, the father ceased his drinking, quietly and humbly gave himself to service through the church to the community, and lived an honorable life for several decades before he died. The son gave a speech at his funeral, honoring the man graciously, living up to his promise to bring honor to the man when he truly deserved it.

I can remember the celebrations after Desert Storm, the conflict to liberate Kuwait from Iran. The people who made sure those soldiers, the newest veterans, were honored, were Vietnam veterans. They were not honored on their return from Southeast Asia, but the Desert Storm veterans surely were. I think the honor they offered brought honor to them.

What to Do

Obviously, give honor when honor is due. How? Testify to the honorable deeds you witness, no matter how small. Commend them before others: that church school teacher; those who raked the church lawn or painted a room or made the coffee; the committee members who accomplished a goal; the givers who brought financial strength to the budget.

Send notes of appreciation, gratitude, and recognition to everyone you can who has done something good. It doesn't have to be anything extremely heroic, but that ounce of honor you bestow will lift the hearts of those who receive it.

Honor the police, fire, and rescue personnel who are, in fact, heroes in our midst. Celebrate the things they have done, the risks they have taken, and the good that they do.

Talent does deserve honor and admiration. I cannot sing well, but I do commend those who do, with my appreciation and gratitude. Unique gifts and individual abilities need encouragement.

Celebrate your mother and father, especially on Mother's Day and Father's Day. But don't be limited to that. Let them know you appreciate their having provided food, shelter, and clothing throughout your childhood, no matter how modest these things were. If they raised you well, honor them for it. The Fifth Commandment promises that by honoring your parents "your days may be long in the land which the Lord your God is giving you" (Exodus 20:12).

"A Scout is trustworthy and honorable." Scouts give badges for achievements they've pursued. There is nothing like a sash full of badges. Like w is e for military personnel. Rank and the pride associated with it merits respect and acknowledgment. Why don't we offer more pins and honors in the church to volunteers? Volunteerism everywhere deserves a special acknowledgment.

"As servants of God, we commend ourselves in every way: through great endurance; in affliction, hardships, and calamities; in beatings, imprisonments, and riots; in labor, sleepless nights, and hunger; by purity, knowledge, patience and kindness; in holiness of spirit and in genuine love; in truthful speech and in the power of God; in the weapons of righteousness for the right hand and for the left; in honor and dishonor, in ill repute and good repute. We are treated as imposters and yet are true; as unknown, and yet are well-known; in dying, and see—we are alive; as punished, and yet not killed; as sorrowful yet always rejoicing; as poor, yet making many rich; as having nothing, and yet possessing everything" (2 Corinthians 6:4-10). In all your ways, no matter what circumstances you endure, be honorable.

A Song

Let us honor the women who've given us birth.
Bless them, Lord, let them inherit the earth.
Bless them with pride and bless them with joy.
Bless them with love from each girl and each boy.
Bless them with wisdom,
Lord, bless them with trust.
Let them be faithful and righteous and just.
Bless them with kindness and bless them with grace.
Let them be fruitful and worthy of praise.

0 Mother, I rested in your tender arm.
You kept me from danger, you kept me from harm.
 You held me and nursed me and smiled when I smiled.
And I want you to know that I'm glad I'm your child.
And I'm glad you're my mother, and I'm glad you've been true.
And I'm glad just to tell you: Mom, I love you.

A Prayer

0 almighty God, to You all honor and glory and praise is due. May we exalt Your name with our words, magnify Your goodness by all our deeds, and dignify Your glory in all the service of our devotion. For You only are honorable; You only are glorious; You only are worthy of praise. We love You, Lord, with all our hearts, and all our minds, and all our strength, and all our souls. In the name of Your glorious and honorable Son, Jesus Christ, our Lord. Amen.

CHAPTER THREE

Whatever is Just

Let justice roll down like waters.
AMOS 5:24

There's a story about an incident that happened concerning the great gates of heaven. One day, some damage occurred when someone broke through the Pearly Gates. The hinges were in disrepair, and the gates became unable to open anymore. St. Peter sought out Satan and told him it was his turn to fix the problem. Satan said he didn't want to. He liked it this way. Peter complained that he was the one who repaired the gates the last time and that long ago, they had made a deal that they would take turns fixing the gates should they break down again.

Satan said, "No. You fix it if you want them to work correctly."

Peter then said, "No ... here's the contract right here. It's binding and unalterable, and if you don't fix things, I'm going to sue."

"Oh, yeah?" said Satan. "Where are you going to find a lawyer?"

What does it mean when we, in our culture, have become able to joke about those who serve justice as though they actually didn't? As though they were unfaithful and couldn't make it to heaven? Does it mean that we believe it? Does it mean that justice has become a joke? Does it reflect a dis-ease among us that reveals a sense that something's just not right? How should we respond when criminals are caught by police and returned so quickly to the streets without paying their dues? Who is responsible for them, anyway? What else can be said when the fact of the matter is that sometimes, crime does pay? It's not supposed to. And what should we think in the light of the prophetic call of Amos to "Let justice roll down like waters, and righteousness like an ever-flowing stream" (5:24)? What about the prophetic claim of Micah, "What does the Lord require of you, but to do justice, and to love kindness, and to walk humbly with your God?" (6:8)?

And consider how true religion has to do with acts of justice in Isaiah 58:6- 11: "Is not this the fast that I choose: to loose the bonds of injustice, to undo the thongs of the yoke, to let the oppressed go free, and to break every yoke? Is it not to share your bread with the hungry, and to bring the homeless poor into your house; when you see the naked, to cover them; and not to hide yourself from your own kin? Then your light shall break forth like the dawn, and your healing shall spring up quickly; your vindicator shall go before you, the glory of the Lord shall be your rear guard. Then you shall call, and the Lord will answer; you shall cry for help and God will say, 'Here I am.' If you remove the yoke from among you, the pointing of the finger, and speaking of evil; if you offer your food the hungry, and satisfy the needs of the afflicted, then shall your light rise in the darkness and your gloom be like the noon-day. And the Lord will guide you continually, and satisfy your needs in parched places, and make your bones strong; and you shall be like a watered garden, like a spring of water whose waters never fail."

Too often, in our culture, we confuse justice with judgment. They are not the same. We do not serve justice simply by handing down a sentence of judgment on those who are guilty. That is only a part of justice. True justice is not completed by punishment, but by correction. Retribution is to be followed by rehabilitation. I am very entertained by vengeance stories. My favorite western movie is *Once Upon a Time in the West (see the story below)*. I love it when the bad guys get their come-uppance, when the drug lord loses everything, when the crime boss ends up in jail. It feels good to see the bad guys brought to justice. But true justice is not served simply by their paying their dues. Many stories have shown how, after people have done their time and are released, they simply return to a life of crime, worse than they were before. Where are the righteous of society during and after the punishment? After retribution has been served? After someone has done their time? Where is all the light of those who claim to possess it, who claim to fight against darkness and would be glad to let their lights shine? Where were they when the guilty people began to stray into the darkness in the first place?

I did my internship in a federal prison in Englewood, Colorado. I was a chaplain-intern: light in the darkness of guilt, shame, denial, and wickedness. One thing I kept wishing for was that there could be a dozen more chaplains. So much more light was needed. But people didn't want to bring it. Maybe they were afraid, or maybe they were indifferent to the need. I visited several parishioners who were in jail. There is no rehabilitation there, but that is where it is most needed. Granted, some reject any efforts of character reform, but these people need help, even when (especially when) they don't think they do.

Proverbs 4:18 says that "the path of the righteous [or just] is like the light of dawn, which shines brighter and brighter until full day." I want to suggest that, in some ways, the fullness of that day has not been reached yet. There's still a lot of darkness, and there are too many people who would rather curse the darkness rather than offer any light for the path forward. But then again, I also believe that the fullness of that day has come. It is now. The light of the world has come. "For it is the God who said, 'Let light shine out of darkness,' who has shone in our hearts" (2 Corinthians 4:6)

Too many people are too willing to sit back, though, and say, "They are not my responsibility." Wrong. Wrong, because the answer to Cain's eternal question (Genesis 4:9), "Am I my brother's keeper?" is "Yes, you are."

Think about what is *just* for a moment. Think about what is right, what is fair, what is moral, what is ethical. Is it just a matter of simply shutting people out when they have gone wrong? Or do the just try to live by faith and, because of faith, love people back to wholeness, lead people back to the light? Is it justice to close ourselves in from the darkness and sit in our comfortable glow of security, while people nearby are desperate and homeless and helpless and angry and empty and hurting? What is justice for them? Justice can be personal, but it is social justice for which we must strive. Justice in the home, the church, the school, the community, the nation, the world.

Is it just or fair for us to spend hundreds of dollars on soft drinks and junk food, when we could (and should) spend at least a little of that for the well-being of others who need good, nutritious food because they don't even have the simple basics for life?

Isaiah said that because we are faithful, we should spend ourselves by pouring ourselves out for the hungry and by satisfying the desires of the afflicted. To me, that includes helping those who have turned to the darkness by finding out what they really need. Do they rob because they are hungry? Do they abuse drugs because they are so hopeless or so lost that they want to escape reality? Are they so low that they can't find a healthy high? Do they abuse the goodness and pleasure of physical intimacy because they are lonely and unloved? Do they live by the pleasure principle (if it feels good, do it)? What about the consequences? What do you think about the people who live for pleasure? How might we be using our resources for our own gratification? How good does it really feel when we have neglected those in need? Do some become violent because they are angry? Are they angry because they are powerless and want to feel powerful somehow? What is the real cause of crime? Isaiah said that we should not get caught up in the pointing of the finger. Our calling is to justice, not to judgment. And even though judgment is a part of justice, it is not all of justice. We should never just overlook the wrong that is done, but we must look beyond it towards setting things right, towards vindication, towards justification. "If you forgive others their trespasses, your heavenly Father will also forgive you. But if you do not forgive others, neither will your Father forgive your trespasses" (Matthew 6:15). There is a sort of karma that comes with justice. The point is obvious: God wants us to be forgiving.

We are all responsible for our own actions because we can choose. We should never excuse our sins because of some past experience that somehow shaped our character and doomed us to behave in some illicit way. By the grace of God, we can choose today what is right to do. "I was born this way" is an excuse that is often used to explain away some sinful choice we make. Well, what if someone claimed that they were born aggressive? Or mean? Or hateful? Does that mean that it's okay to be violent? No. Such behavior is often corrected. Or at least we often attempt to correct it. Sin is often a matter of behavior, and we can choose to behave in sinful ways or not. We have free will.

Apply this to social justice. We shouldn't perpetuate unfair practices simply because that's the way things have always been. Collectively, we can change; we can choose the way we want things to be. Take poverty, for example. No one chooses to be poor, but we need to support the changes that will break the cycles of social practice that keep people in their place. Create opportunities, offer possibilities, and develop the chances that give people the breaks they need that will raise them from their circumstances. Take advantage of those opportunities and seek out those possibilities. Never feel as though your circumstances can never change. Let the scriptures be your guide. Too many people respond to the

Word of God as if it didn't apply to them. They tend to justify themselves rather than God (Job 32:2).

All believers should, by their calling, defend the Word rather than just defend themselves. If you or someone you know is living in a manner that is contrary to God's Word, by behaving in a way condemned by scripture, don't suggest that the scriptures are wrong. That just adds insult to injury. To water down the authority of scripture is to make the Word of God null and void. And we end up making our own rules. We become our own authority. When God condemns greed, for example, that means we shouldn't be greedy. When God condemns adultery that means we should not be adulterous. Why should we ever make excuses for sins upon which God has pronounced judgment? Justice is a process of justifying God. Yes, God is merciful, but as with the woman caught in adultery, we are to "go, and sin no more" (John 8:11).

Mercy. When you think of justice, do you ever think of mercy? Too often, our focus is on retribution or revenge, while we, who are followers of Christ, should be more focused on mercy. "Blessed are the merciful, for they shall receive mercy" (Matthew 5:7). Listen to Paul's appeal in Romans 12:9-21: "Let love be genuine. Hate what is evil; hold fast to what is good. Love one another with mutual affection. Outdo one another in showing honor. Do not lag in zeal, be ardent in spirit, and serve the Lord. Rejoice in hope, be patient in suffering, persevere in prayer. Contribute to the needs of the saints; extend hospitality to strangers. Bless those who persecute you; bless and do not curse them. Rejoice with those who rejoice, weep with those who weep. Live in harmony with one another. Do not be haughty, but associate with the lowly. Do not claim to be wiser than you are. Do not repay anyone evil for evil, but give thought for what is noble in the sight of all. If possible, so far as it depends on you, live peaceably with all. Beloved, never avenge yourselves, but leave room for the wrath of God, for it is written, 'Vengeance is mine, I will repay, says the Lord.' No, 'if your enemy is hungry, feed them; if they are thirsty, give them something to drink; for by so doing this you will heap burning coals on their heads.' Do not be overcome by evil, but overcome evil with good."

And again, from 1 Thessalonians 5:15: "See that none of you repays evil for evil, but always seek to do good to one another and to all."

When justice rolls, righteousness flows, if we let it. That includes showing mercy.

We get too caught up in our fallen human desire to retaliate, exact revenge, and get even. We want retribution, reciprocation, and restitution. What is needed is vindication, reformation, and reparations. Jesus repudiated the notion of retaliation: "You have heard that it was said, 'An eye for an eye, and a tooth for a tooth.' But I say to you, do not resist an evildoer: but if anyone strikes you on the right cheek, turn the other also" (Matthew 5:38-39).

So what should we do? John the Baptist said, "Whosoever has two coats must share with anyone who has none. And whoever has food must do likewise" (Luke 3:11). The faithful have hearts that can overflow. And because of faith, the faithful can even make a few sacrifices! Is it a sacrifice to show mercy? I love what Paul said at the beginning of Romans 12: "Do not be conformed to this world, but be transformed by the renewing of your minds" (verse 2). By the grace of the

Holy Spirit, we can change the way we think. We need to change the way we think.

Edmund Burke said thar the only thing necessary for evil to triumph is for good people to do nothing. That, I believe, is what is happening all around us. Too much nothing is being done. I believe that for every single person who goes astray, at least ten good people are needed to lead them back to the path of righteousness. So ... where are you going to find ten good people? The harsh reality is that maybe for every one person who goes astray, there are perhaps a few dozen self-righteous "good" people just pointing the finger of blame, of judgment, of shame; the way they did with the woman who was caught in an act of adultery (John 8:3-11). The sad reality is that it is probably truer that, for every ten lost souls, there is only one good person trying to offer any guidance and direction, any light. Even that may be generous.

What good does it do to sit back and say that the woman caught in adultery deserved the humiliation? What good does it do to think about the wicked conditions surrounding those in prison and say, "They deserve it"? Such an attitude never made anyone a better person. What is it that these people deserve from Jesus Christ, who came to seek and to save the lost? (Luke 19:10). What is it they deserve from His followers? The Spirit of Christ dwells in those who believe in Him. We should be like Him.

Isn't it our purpose, our calling in faith, to end the cycles of desperation, to break the yoke of oppression, the yoke that weighs on the shoulders that carry the burden of sin, guilt, and shame; of poverty, desperation, and need; of temptation, evil, and weakness? We need to see that when we help the least and lost, we are doing it for Christ (Matthew 25:40). We need to think beyond the letter of the law and catch the spirit of the law.

And guilt does not carry over from generation to generation. Though we are all sinners because we are born into a fallen world, I am not a sinner because of my parents. I will grant that wicked fathers and mothers can greatly influence wicked behavior in their children. The sour grapes that were eaten by our parents do not set their children's teeth on edge, though. They do not have to make them bitter or leave a bad taste in their mouths. They can, but they don't have to. Ultimately, we are only accountable for our own sins. The faithful, however, can 1) help people break out of the cycles of brokenness, and 2) not pour automatic judgment on others simply because they are broken. "'Behold, all lives are mine,' says the Lord" (Ezekiel 18:4). "In those days they shall no longer say, 'The parents have eaten sour grapes, and the children's teeth are set on edge.' But all shall die for their own sin; the teeth of everyone who eats the sour grapes, shall be set on edge" (Jeremiah 31:29; see also Ezekiel 18:2-3)."Parents shall not be put to death for their children, nor shall children be put to death for their parents; only for their own crimes may persons be put to death" (Deuteronomy 24:16). Yes, death is, in fact, a consequence of sin because "sin, when it is fully grown, gives birth to death" (James 1:15). Sin does not need to be perpetuated, because the light of righteousness can dawn to interrupt the downward spiral. People can change the path they're on because the faithful can lead them rightly, in truth, with hope, through love.

Justice. Justification. Being right with God. Personal justice is being made right (righteous) with Go d. Social justice is when we are all right with God. We believe in justice. Peace with justice. There is no peace until we are all truly right with God. It may seem impossible at times, but ... it is our purpose, our calling. We need to be peacemakers by working for justice. Start with yourself.

It is said that justice is blind. It *should* be. It should be impartial, with no regard for race, or gender, or age, or wealth. The problem, however, is that we are not blind. We all face justice with preconceived notions that often put weight in the balance against truth. An important exercise of faith is to think about those attitudes and preconceived notions that we might have in our own lives. People are often raised with prejudices and preferences, but we need to see beyond them. We need to see how the world into which we are brought has well-established attitudes about certain things. I was raised to be a Cubs fan. But because my friend was a Sox fan, I realized, as a kid, that it was all right to root for the Sox too. Of course, we all need to realize that we are not saved by being a fan of a certain team. I am not saved by my heritage, or my color, or my wealth, or my height, or my gender, or any other accident of my condition. "As many of you as were baptized into Christ have clothed yourselves with Christ. There is no longer Jew or Greek, there is no longer slave or free, there is no longer male and female; for all of you are one in Christ Jesus" (Galatians 3:27-28).

Paul repeats the famous proverbial truth first proclaimed by Habakkuk (2:4), that "the one who is righteous shall live by faith" (Romans 1:17). He says it again in Galatians 3:11.

And it is said again in Hebrews 10:38. We are not saved because we can condemn someone else. That saves no one. And it serves no one, in a positive way. We are not saved because we are morally straight, or proud, or innocent, or good. We are saved by faith. And because we are faithful, we will be righteous, we will do good, we will serve God.

And we can best serve God by serving some of God's other children.

Think about what is just. Not only what is just in your own, individual life, but what is just in God's good world. If you look out and see a lack of justice where it ought to be, you will know where you can serve. Let your thoughts about what is just be like roots. And let your actions be their fruits. "You will know them by their fruits" (Matthew 7:20).

So think about what is just. But don't just think; be fruitful. When justice rolls, righteousness flows. And that includes mercy.

To inspire you to think about whatever is just, study what is in the scriptures:

"As for you, return to your God; hold fast to love and justice, and wait continually for your God" (Hosea 12:6).

"When justice is done, it is a joy to the righteous, but dismay to evildoers" (Proverbs 21: 15).

"Depart from evil and do good; so shall you will abide in forever. For the LORD loves justice and will not forsake his faithful ones. The righteous shall be kept safe forever, but the children of the wicked shall be cut off"(Psalm 37:27-29).

"God has told you, O mortal, what is good. And what does the LORD require of you but to do justice and to love kindness and to walk humbly with your God?" (Micah 6:8).

"Learn to do good; seek justice; rescue the oppressed; defend the orphan; plead for the widow" (Isaiah 1:17).

"Happy are those who observe justice, who do righteousness at all times" (Psalm 106:3).

"You shall not render an unjust judgment; you shall not be partial to the poor or defer to the great; with justice you shall judge your neighbor" (Leviticus 19: 15).

"Listen to me, my people; and give heed to me, my nation: for a teaching will go out from me; and my justice for a light to the peoples. I will bring near my deliverance swiftly, my salvation has gone out, and my arms will rule the peoples. The coastlands wait for me, and for my arm they hope" (Isaiah 51:4-5).

"When Gentiles, who do not possess the Law, do instinctively what Law requires, these, though not having the Law, are a law to themselves" (Romans 2:14-15).

"My friends, if someone is detected in a transgression, you who have received the Spirit should restore such a one in a spirit of gentleness. Take care that you yourselves are not tempted. Bear one another's burdens, and in this way you will fulfill the law of Christ" (Galatians 6:1-2).

"His authority shall grow continually, and there shall be endless peace for the throne of David and his kingdom. He will establish and uphold it with justice and righteousness from this time onward and forevermore. The zeal of the LORD of hosts will do this (Isaiah 9:7).

"Cursed be anyone who deprives the alien, the orphan, and the widow of justice" (Deuteronomy 27:19).

Stories

"The scribes and the Pharisees brought a woman who had been caught in adultery. And making her stand before all of them, they said to Him, 'Teacher, this woman was caught in the very act of committing adultery. Now in the Law Moses commanded us to stone such women. Now what do you say?' They said this to test Him, so they might have some charge to bring against Him. Jesus bent down and wrote with his finger on the ground. When they kept questioning Him, He straightened up and said to them, 'Let anyone among you who is without sin be the first to throw a stone at her.' And once again he bent down and wrote on the ground. When they heard it, they away one by one, beginning with the elders; and Jesus was left alone with the woman standing before Him. Jesus straightened up and said to her, 'Woman, where are they? Has no one condemned you?' She said, 'No one, sir.' And Jesus said, 'Neither do I condemn you. Go your way, and from now on do not sin again'" (John 8:3- 11).

"Jesus told them a parable about their need to pray always and not to lose heart. He said: 'In a certain city there was a judge who neither feared God nor had respect for people. In that city there was a widow who kept coming to him and saying, "Grant me justice against my opponent." For a while he refused; but later he said to himself, "Though I have no fear God and no respect for anyone, yet because this widow keeps bothering me, I will grant her justice, so that she may not wear me out by continually coming!" And the Lord said, 'Listen to what the unjust judge says. And will not God grant justice to his chosen ones who cry out to him day and night? Will he delay long in helping them? I tell you, he will quickly grant justice to them. And yet, when the Son of Man comes, will he find faith on the earth?'" (Luke 18: 1-8).

"If another member of the church sins against you, go and point out the fault, when the two of you are alone. If the member listens to you, you have regained that one. But if you are not listened to, take one or two others along with you, so that every word may be confirmed by the evidence of two or three witnesses. If the member refuses to listen to them, tell it to the church; and if the offender refuses to listen even to the church, let such a one be to you as a Gentile and a tax collector" (Matthew 18:15- 17).

"For this reason the kingdom of heaven may be compared to a king who wished to settle accounts with his slaves. When he began the reckoning, one who owed him ten thousand talents was brought to him; and as he could not pay, his lord ordered him to be sold, together with his wife and his children and all his possessions, and payment be made. So the slave fell on his knees before him, saying, 'Have patience with me, and I will repay you everything.' And out of pity for him, the lord of that slave released him and forgave him the debt. But the same slave, as he went out, came upon one of his fellow slaves who owed him a hundred denarii; and seizing him by the throat, he said, 'Pay what you owe.' Then the fellow slave fell down and pleaded with him, 'Have patience with me, and I will pay you.' But he refused; then he went and threw him into prison until he would pay the debt. When his fellow slaves saw what had happened, they were greatly distressed, and they went and reported to their lord all that had taken place. Then his lord summoned him and said to him, 'You wicked slave! I forgave you all that debt because you pleaded with me. Should you not have had mercy on your fellow slave, as I had mercy on you?' And in anger his lord handed him over to be tortured until he would pay his entire debt. So my heavenly Father will also do to every one of you, if you do not forgive your brother or sister from your heart"(Matthew 18:23- 35).

"You have heard that it was said to those of ancient times, 'You shall not murder;' and 'whoever murders shall be liable to judgment.' But I say to you that if you are angry with a brother or sister, you will be liable to judgment; and if you insult your brother or sister, you will be liable to the council; and if you say, 'You fool!' will be liable to the hell of fire. So when you are offering your gift at the altar, if you remember that your brother or sister has something against you, leave your gift there before the altar and go; first be reconciled to your brother or sister, and then come and offer your gift. Come to terms quickly with your accuser while you are going with him to court, lest your accuser may hand you over to the judge, and the judge to the guard, and you will be thrown into prison. Truly, I tell you, you will never get out until you have paid the last penny" (Matthew 5:21-26).

Christ is saying, in part, that we need to make things right with others before we can be right with God by offering a gift at the altar. If we are not right with others, we are probably not right with God. Justification, being justified (made right) with God, begins with being made right (making things right) with others.

Once upon a Time in the West is the best western movie ever. The background is the development of the early railroad in the American West. Henry Fonda plays the baddest bad guy you can imagine. He works for an unscrupulous railroad mogul and eliminates people who are in the way. Charles Bronson plays a man out for vengeance. As a boy of about nine or ten, his family was in the way, and Henry Fonda and gang eliminated them. Bronson, as a boy, was made to stand, hands tied behind his back, with his older brother, standing on his shoulders, hands tied behind his back too, but with his neck in a noose ... in the hot desert sun. Bronson couldn't hold up after so long. His brother knew this and with his feet pushed him over, knowing he would be strangled to death in the noose. Long story short: years later, as a man, Charles Bronson finally avenges his brother and family by killing Henry Fonda in a gunfight. I love the movie because you just want Henry Fonda to get what's coming to him. But this is *not* justice.

In the science fiction tales of *Star Trek*, there is a principle called "the Prime Directive." Essentially, the Prime Directive is "do not interfere, or interrupt, or influence in any way, shape, or form, the progress (or the lack of progress) of primitive cultures on planets that are not in the United Federation of Planets and that have not yet developed interplanetary travel." In other words, let them grow at their own pace, develop at their own rate, and learn from their own mistakes.

In an episode of Star Trek: The Next Generation, while exploring another solar system, the android Data was able to isolate and understand a weak radio transmission that asked, "Is anybody out there?" And he responded by saying, "Yes." In a short amount of time, Data learned that the world he was communicating with was falling apart. There were so many earthquakes, and so much volcanic activity, that all life on the planet was doomed to perish in a very short time.

The debate in Captain Picard's ready room with his senior officers ranged from "should we intervene and save this planet from destruction?" to "we should not interrupt the evolution of things and allow the people to perish." Knowing the pain and suffering the people and creatures of this planet were condemned to go through turned the debate into an emotional one rather than one of pure logical reasoning. On the one hand, if it is wrong to just allow anyone to suffer, and we have the means to prevent it, we ought to help. On the other hand, to disregard the Prime Directive would be to disobey Starfleet Command's number one principle.

As the argument developed, the question of fate entered into the discussion. If it is this world's fate to erupt into a planet uninhabitable for its contemporary life-forms, then we should not interfere. But then again, it was also fate that enabled Data to pick up the plea transmitted into space, and it was fate that brought their ship into this galaxy. Perhaps fate was leading the crew of the *Enterprise* to the rescue.

Their final decision: rescue the planet.

Brothers and sisters, the prime directive for Christians could very easily be: anyone who knows the right to do and fails to do it, commits sin (James 4:17).

First of all, we do not live by fate but by faith.

Second, we *can* know what to do. How do we know what to do? By knowing what we would wish for if we put ourselves in someone else's place. What James has said is a restating of Matthew 7:12: "In everything, do to others as you would have them do to you." The Golden Rule: our prime directive. Meanwhile, whoever knows what is right to do and fails to do it, for them it is sin.

How do we know? By putting ourselves there, into that situation, as if it were happening to us. This is what we respond to. This compels us to act. This way, what we do becomes a personal thing. Very personal. We empathize with others. We sympathize. We can feel what others might feel, and we feel it with them. They are not alone. And we cannot, should not, isolate ourselves. Justice.

My father-in -law would often attend cocktail parties where some of the people acted a bit snobbishly. When asked what he did for a living, Bob, who worked for Commonwealth Edison, would sometimes tell people he was a garbage man and watch those snobs begin to look at him and treat him very condescendingly. Status prejudice. Injustice. An attitude changes was called for.

Those in power sometimes (often?) serve power more than they serve justice. The story of Pontius Pilate serves as a good example of this: "Pilat e said to the Chief Priests and the crowds, 'I find no basis for an accusation against this man'" (Luke 23:4).

"I have examined Hirn in your presence and have not found this man guilty of any of your charges against him. Neither has Herod ... Indeed he has done nothing to deserve death"(Luke 23:14-15).

"Pilate tried to release Him, but the Jews cried out, 'If you release this man, you are no friend of the emperor'" (John 19: 12).

Not justice.

But Pilate could have served justice.

A man once blamed the darkness on the failure of the sun, rather than on the coming of the clouds. The sun was still shining, but clouds can darken its light, or perhaps you have turned away from its light. A person doesn't lose sight of the sun all at once. First, the wind may change. Then clouds will come, only a few at first. Then, more frequently, thicker and thicker. Soon the man forgets that the sun is there at all. And he blames the sun for having left him. Don't blame the sun for your darkness.

What to Do

Examine yourself. Do you feel inferior or superior to others simply because of your race, your stature, your gender, your heritage, your wealth, or your poverty? Face seriously Paul's correction of such an attitude in Galatians 3:2 7- 28: "All of you are one in Christ Jesus."

Remember the atoning work of Jesus Christ. He died to atone for my sins. I do not receive what I deserve for my sins because He took them upon Himself and died for me. Justice is merciful.

What is fair? Is it fair that you were born with privileges based on race or gender or a heritage of wealth, while others were born into poverty and a culture that perpetuates prejudices against your race? Of course it isn't. But if you are aware of these realities, you may know that you have attitudes to overcome. To overcome, change your attitude, and work to change your culture by testifying to your awareness and change. For example, if you feel as though you need to behave a certain way just to fit in, something needs to change.

Think globally and act locally. Not a new idea, but the point to be made is that we can't work for justice simply by thinking about what is wrong with the world. Saying, "It's the system," is a way to relinquish responsibility to act. Too often, we think about justice in the abstract and then fail to do anything concrete. For example, pollution: clean up your location. Be part of an Adopt-a-Highway effort. Encourage your company, business, or school to practice good stewardship of the environment. Drive less, and use public transportation more. Be sure your car gets good gas mileage and is a minimum polluter. Meanwhile, work to change the culture in which you live. Regulations that protect the atmosphere, land, and waters need to be enforced; research whatever watchdogs might be holding those accountable to such regulations and support them, work with them, and magnify their voice.

Stand up for those who are treated unfairly. Defend them when they are honorable. If someone else deserves a raise before you do, and you know it, encourage those in charge to be just, to do what is right. Likewise, do your best to promote equal pay for equal work among all employees.

Bullying. Everyone is against it. But what can you do? Support anti- bullying programs, and obviously, if you are aware of bullying or unwanted behavior (especially sexual), speak up.

Affirmative action. By encouraging and validating employment for those who come from backgrounds that have been systematically disadvantaged, we generate both fairness and justice.

Obey the law. This should go without saying. But we all need to live by the standards set before us. Change laws that need changing. Work to open the doors of the system that seem to close doors for some. Remember the civil rights movement of the 1960s? People realized the unfairness of many laws that perpetuated racial and gender discrimination, and protested and petitioned for change. Many changes happened. Many are still needed.

The environment. Take care of this planet. Be a good steward of earth's resources. Do not be wasteful or destructive. Recycle, encourage recycling, and encourage leaders to develop policies that protect the land, the waters, and the atmosphere. It would be an injustice against those who live downstream to poison the stream here simply because the toxins are carried away. Generations yet to come are downstream from us today.

Us and them. Do not picture the world as us and them, but as one great fellowship of love throughout the whole wide earth. In Christ, there is no East or West.

A Song: We Hear Your Spirit Calling

>Tune: "Londonderry Aire"

0 Lord our God, we hear Your Spirit calling
>for us to go and tell what we believe.

Your kingdom's come, with all Your blessings falling
>upon the hearts of all who would receive.

How wonderful the message of Your story;
>your words of love, of goodness, peace and grace.

And we will share the promise of Your glory
>and of the hope, the hope to see You face to face.

0 Lamb of God, 0 Carpenter from Nazareth,
>You came to make the perfect sacrifice.

Your Blood was shed, and You redeemed us by Your Death.
>And for our sins You paid the final price.

So long ago, with fishermen beside the sea,
>the time had come to cast their nets anew.

So, now as then, the calling comes to you and me
>to draw the hearts, the hearts of all the whole world through.

A Prayer

0 Lord, open my eyes that I may see the needs of others; open my ears that I may hear their cries; and open my heart so that they may never be without care. Let me never be afraid to defend the weak because of a fear of the strong nor afraid to defend the poor because of the resentment of the rich nor afraid

to defend persons of another race because of the prejudice of some. Show me where love and justice and hope are needed, and use me to bring my faith to the wants of all who lack the peace of righteousness. So open my mind that my hands will open, and I may do some work of peace in the name of Jesus Christ. Amen.

CHAPTER FOUR

Whatever is Pure

> God did not call us to impurity, but in holiness.
> 1 THESSALONIANS 4:7

"I do not understand my own actions. For I do not do what I want, but I do the very thing I hate.... For if I do not do the good I want, but the evil I do not want is what I do.... I see in my members another law at war with the law of my mind, making me captive to the law of sin" (Romans 7:15, 19, 23).

Paul struggled hard to overcome his inner conflicts. So must we. Paul had hope, though. Half the battle is fought by discovering what is sinful in us, or as he said, "It was sin, working death in me through what is good, in order that sin might be shown to be sin" (Romans 7:13). Sin must be recognized as sin before it can be forgiven. But forgiveness cannot come until there is repentance. And repentance cannot happen until there is a confession of sin. And it all begins by the grace of God working in us "through what is good."

I believe Paul summed up the problem of our fallen human nature well when he said, "So then, with my mind I am a slave to the law of God, but with my flesh, I am a slave to the law of sin" (Romans 7:25). But there is hope. Paul goes on to proclaim:

> There is therefore now no condemnation for those who are in Christ Jesus. For the law of the Spirit of life in Christ Jesus has set me free from the law of sin and death! For God has done what the Law, weakened by the flesh, could not do: by sending His own Son in the likeness of sinful flesh, and to deal with sin, He condemned sin in the flesh, so that the just requirement of the Law might be fulfilled in us, who walk not according to the flesh but according to the Spirit. To set the mind on the flesh is death, but to set the mind on the Spirit is life and peace. For this reason the mind that is set on the flesh is hostile to God; it does not submit to God's law, indeed it cannot; and those who are in the flesh cannot please God. But you are not in the flesh, you are in the Spirit, since the Spirit of God dwells in you. (Romans 8:1-9 a)

"Those who live according to the Spirit set their minds on the things of the Spirit" (8:5b). What are the things of the Spirit? Paul gives us a clue:

> Whatever is true,
> whatever is honorable,
> whatever is just,
> whatever is pure,
> whatever is pleasing,
> whatever is gracious,
> if there is any excellence,
> if there is anything worthy of praise,
> think about these things.
> (PHILIPPIANS 4:8)

Consider in the present context, the context Paul alludes to when he mentions the war of the mind and the flesh; the context alluded to in Genesis 6:5-6 when "the Lord saw that the wickedness of humankind was great in the earth, and that every inclination of the thoughts of their hearts was only evil continually. And the Lord was sorry that He had made humankind on the earth, and it grieved Him to His heart." Consider from this context: whatever is pure. Consider not only the things that are pure, but also consider the practice of purity.

First of all, the things that are pure: innocence, guiltlessness, sinlessness, things that are undefiled, unadulterated, and uncorrupt; consider these things. What are they? Let these things be the things on your mind, the thoughts in your heart, the objects of your contemplation. Let them be your soul's desire, not only for you to experience for yourself, but to witness in others. Even though you have been impure, you can experience purity. Our minds are sometimes filled with so much garbage, so many degrading images, and so many unclean ideas that we can be contaminated. We can become so preoccupied with such distortions that our souls become depraved and our lifestyles turn toward decadence. At times, our behavior becomes just plain wicked because of our thoughts. It seems that so few people dwell upon the purity among us and within us that it becomes forgotten. Does it even exist? Is it out there somewhere? And just as much as impure water can spread disease, impure thoughts can spread corruption.

People spend a lot of time and effort making a big deal about guilt, especially the guilt of others, and sometimes their own guilt. Because of this, little effort is spent considering the innocence that is in their lives also. It is there by the grace of God. We remember each other's sins and forget each other's gifts. It's like straining at gnats and swallowing camels (Matthew 23:24). Too often, we disregard what is really important when we notice the blemish and deny the beauty still there.

Long, long ago, there was such a thing as ritual purity. It had to do with clean and unclean things. There was a religious code that required the faithful to stay away from what was considered to be unclean. And though there is something to be said for cleanliness, cleanliness is not godliness. It may be nearby, even right next to it, but something is lacking if all you've got is cleanliness while godliness is the goal. It takes more than outward purity to be godly. Jesus said that it is the pure of heart who are truly blessed. Their blessing is that they would see God (Matthew 5:8).

It may seem unusual to imagine that purity is something that can be practiced. Most of the time, we think of things as either being pure or impure. But many things are not made pure; they are purified. And the practice of purity is the process of purification. The psalmist said, "Create in me a clean heart, 0 God, and put a new and right spirit within me"(Psalm 51:10).

But you wouldn't ask God for a clean heart unless you were aware of the fact that it is defiled. You wouldn't ask God for a new and right spirit unless you were aware of the fact that something is wrong. The first step in the practice of purity is self-examination. Look hard at your life. Is there anything wrong with it? Is it less than perfect? Are there any flaws or faults? Any errors? Is there any tension or brokenness? Is there guilt or self-righteousness? When I say self-righteousness, are there any people in the world you might consider unworthy of your graciousness? Are there any neighbors, relatives, or friends you are unable to associate with, among whom you feel uncomfortable? Because if there are, well then, what makes you so great? Aren't you just a wonderful hypocrite? Don't you feel that God has the ability to give them a new and right spirit too? We notice the blemish and forget the beauty.

Examine yourself. Search yourself. Look at your past. Are there any grudges you hold or that are held against you? Is there anything you've done or neglected doing for which you are sorry? Name them to yourself. Doing so will hurt, but there is hope; this chapter's not over yet. We've only just begun the practice of purification.

Now, name them to God. The second step in the practice of purity, the process of purification, is confession. Confession is more than just admitting you are a sinner. If that was all it was, they'd call it "admission." Confession is more than acknowledging what is wrong or sinful in your life. Confession is an unmasking, a disclosure, or uncovering. To confess is not only to open up, but to own up. Yes, it may make you feel exposed and vulnerable, but remember, God is in this process, and God is watching over you (not just watching you); God is protecting you. Realize that too many people try to disown their problems, their sins. We try to project what is wrong with our lives or what is hurting us, elsewhere, sometimes onto other people, sometimes onto the system, passing the blame on to someone or something else or shirking the blame by claiming, "That's just the way things are," or "That's just the way I am." But what about that new and right spirit? Where does that come in?

Now, I don't believe that in order to confess, we need to broadcast or publish anything. If that was the case, God would still provide a retraction for us. But I like the idea of owning up. Once we can truly own our problems, errors, sins, trespasses, we can begin to truly deal with them. And it is God we must first deal with, not with an earthly confessor, although a friend, counselor, or pastor can help us and guide us onward, encouraging us and standing by our side. We may need such a someone because we might just continue to project our problems elsewhere or end up wallowing in our grief. Grief is good: "Blessed are those who mourn for they shall be comforted" (Matthew 5:4). But wallowing in guilt never improved anything. Or we might fall short of owning up to the whole problem.

Nonetheless, confession is an important part of the practice of purity.

Now, what do we do once the problem is owned and confessed? We are not saved by confessing our sins. We are not done simply when it's all been laid on the table (or altar). This leads us to the next step: repentance. And to repent is more, much more than saying, "I'm sorry," or, "All right, I won't do it anymore," or, "Well, I'm sure glad I got that off my chest." Though confession may be very cathartic, repentance leads to absolution, forgiveness, release.

Sure, it's good to get it off your chest, out of your heart. You feel unburdened. Now you have a clean heart. But that's because, now, it's in God's hands too. Notice I say that it is in God's hands too. You and God are carrying it together now. But it's not gone until you completely let go. And it is not finally gone until God lets go. Of course, God doesn't really hold on to our sins. God is removing our sins from us. And ultimately, there will be a change.

The first part of repentance is regret. In biblical times, this feeling about sin was expressed by rending their clothes, wearing sackcloth, covering themselves with ashes, and mourning: "Blessed are those who mourn, they will be comforted" (Matthew 5:4). People looked penitent. People acted penitential. Today, in our Western culture, we tend to intellectualize about our feelings rather than to express them so boldly. But it's all right to grieve our sins. In 2 Corinthians 7:10-11, Paul said, "Godly grief produces a repentance that leads to salvation and brings no regret, but worldly grief produces death. For see what earnestness this godly grief has produced in you: what eagerness to clear yourselves, what indignation, what alarm, what longing, what zeal, what punishment. At every point you have proved yourselves guiltless in this matter." Paul saw a whole process unfold as his friends grieved after he pointed out some faults. They came around and proved themselves guiltless. It's all right to feel hurt by our sins, by what makes you (and God) sad. God was regretful, "grieved to His heart" when He saw human wickedness multiplying among His Creation (Genesis 6:6). But we are not done repenting just because we are sorry. That godly sorrow leads us to want something else: joy. But joy is not automatic.

From regret, we progress to removal. We remove the sin, that dirt, that evil. We throw it away, cast it off. After the sackcloth and ashes, they would begin to wash. We remove the dirt by cleansing, by pouring something clean and pure over us. By diving deep into the truth and then rising, raising our heads again, intending never again to sink into the mire of sin. Here is where removal can happen by crowding the evil out. Fill your mind with so much good that there will be no room for evil. Immerse yourself in the scriptures and study hard. Learn the good you need to know. Follow the way with expediency, and you will know the paths of righteousness as well as the best.

Once the sin has been removed from us-God will remove it "as far as the east is from the west" (Psalm 103:12)-we must then return. "In returning and rest you shall be saved; in quietness and in trust shall be your strength" (Isaiah 30:15). To what do we return? We return to faith. We return to where we belong: under the power and authority of God. By grace, we return to a life of grace. New clothes would replace the sackcloth. We would receive "a new and right spirit within" (Psalm 51: 10b). Paul would call believers to a change of clothing: "You were taught to put away your former way of life, your old self, corrupt and deluded by its lusts, and to be renewed in the Spirit of your minds; and to clothe yourselves with the new self, created according to the likeness of God in true righteousness and holiness" (Ephesians 4:22- 24). Not only that, but Paul would have us put on the armor of God (Ephesians 6:10-18). Meanwhile, at the point of our turning, God throws off the burden we have unloaded, and we are forgiven.

Worthy of noting, here, is that the word translated repent is metanoia, which literally means "change of mind." To repent is to change our minds, to begin thinking differently.

Many people never completely change when they begin repenting or begin following Christ. To truly repent is to change your ways, change the way we think.

Finally, repentance is completed by faith. We "go ... and do not sin again." Sadly, though, as often as not, a person's repentance is not complete. We haven't really changed our direction because we haven't changed our ways. We may say we are sorry, but then we return to the same crowd that tempted us to sin in the first place. Please realize, though, that being tempted is not a sin. Even Jesus was tempted, but He defended Himself with the truth of scripture (Matthew 4:1-11).

We fall short of the purity at which we aim in the practice of purification because we do not learn to change our lifestyles when we change the way we think. The practice of purity is not a onetime thing. It is ongoing, never-ending, and perpetual. That's why it is completed by faith: faithful living. Don't expect to feel pure and be pure in just one day. It can happen. People can be completely changed by the grace of God. But it often takes years of constant vigil, a whole lifetime of changing. We don't become great musicians by not practicing. Lots and lots of practice makes even the hardest score natural for a good musician. Gymnasts may make their motions look easy, but they spent months building the strength and skill to do what they do. Likewise, self-examination, confession, and repentance must be practiced all the time. Remember that we live in a fallen world. It's not always a very clean place. When we get some dirt on us, we need to wash. Every time we get dirty, we need cleansing.

Don't let yourself become so dirty that you become offensive. Be honorable.

A word about guilt seems relevant here. Guilt can haunt us. It can darken our hearts and spoil our enjoyment of life. David, the psalmist, felt such a struggle:

When I kept silence, my body wasted away through my groaning all day long. For day and night your hand was heavy on me; my strength was dried up as by the heat of summer. (Psalm 32:3-4)

Sleepless nights, moral anguish, tight-jawed remorse can often get the better of us, and we suffer. But there is good news:

Then I acknowledged my sin to you and I did not hide my iniquity. I said, "I will confess my transgressions to the LORD." And you forgave the guilt of my sin. (Psalm 32:5)

David was so relieved as he confessed, repented, and found forgiveness that he actually began this psalm by saying:

Happy are those whose transgression is forgiven, whose sin is covered. Happy are those to whom the Lord imputes no iniquity, and in whose spirit is no deceit. (Psalm 32:1-2)

Still, guilt can be tricky. I felt guilty a few days ago when I didn't get my workout in. I gave myself a serious guilt trip, haunted by my need to lose weight, knowing I would feel better for having at least stretched my muscles and wanting to be healthy. Of course, I didn't really lose any sleep over not exercising. Paul Tournier, a psychologist, in a wonderful book entitled Guilt and Grace, distinguished between true guilt and false guilt, acknowledging how we sometimes feel guilty when, really, we've done nothing morally wrong. And though there can be a sin of neglect, which leaves us feeling guilty, we need to discern the difference.

I feel uneasy at being in good health when there are so many people sick; happy, when there are so many people unhappy; at having money when so many people are short of it. I feel a certain discomfort too at having an interesting vocation when so many people sigh beneath the burden of a job they hate; and even at having been taken hold of by God and illuminated by faith, when so many people suffer in anguish, isolation and obscurity!

Although remorseful over the fact that he has so much while he sees how others might be lacking, he later says, "It is precisely because I am acutely aware of our guilt in all its extent that I am also acutely aware of grace, which is our sole help."

Indeed, so much of life has the tone of a guilt trip, and so many sermons may hammer away at guilt, that we almost get the impression that we are supposed to feel guilty. Paul did say, "No one is righteous! No, not even one" (Romans 3:10). Jesus even said, "Truly, I tell you, just as you did not do it to one of the least of these, you did not do it to me" (Matthew 25:45). And they are condemned for what they didn't do. His parable of the great judgment needs to be seen as a warning, compelling us to do our part to feed the hungry, help the thirsty, welcome the stranger, clothe the naked, tend the sick, and care for those in prison. But unless we are woefully neglectful, I think feeling guilty for what we have left undone is not healthy. Neglect can be a sin, and we do need to repent and be forgiven when we are neglectful, but a healthy faith hears, with David, "Happy are those whose transgression is forgiven, whose sin is covered." And that can happen as we repent. The message of guilt must be tempered by the goodness of grace.

Still guilt comes. It comes when we fall short of thinking about these things. It comes when we know that we cannot live up to the ideals we have. It comes when we have to face up to and be accountable for our own hypocrisy. The thoughts that enter our minds may sometimes even contradict the Christian mind. But we also know that God isn't finished with any of us yet. Maybe some of us still have a long way to go. I sure do. But we need to "work out our own salvation with fear and trembling, for it is God who works in you to will and to work to His good pleasure" (Philippians 2:1 2- 13). And it is work. Some people have to work very hard to deal with their guilt.

I will grant that the practice of purity can take a great deal of mental and emotional effort, at least at first. But wouldn't the blessing of the vision be worth it to become pure in heart? Especially when the vision is a vision of God?

God's divine power has given us everything needed for life and godliness, through the knowledge of Him who called us by His own glory and goodness. Thus He has given us, through these things, His precious and very great promises, so that through them you may escape from the corruption that is in the world because of lust, and may become participants of the divine nature. For this very reason, you must make every effort to support your faith with goodness, and goodness with knowledge, and knowledge with self-control, and self-control with endurance, and endurance with godliness, and godliness with mutual affection, and mutual affection with love. For if these things are yours and are increasing among you, they keep you from being ineffective and unfruitful in the knowledge of our Lord Jesus Christ" (2 Peter 1:3-8).

Godliness. God's divine power has granted to us all things that pertain to godliness. We can escape from the corruption that's in the world. We can become partakers of the divine nature. We are not saved by our purity; we are saved by faith alone. But faith naturally magnifies itself by supplementing itself with virtue: the virtue of purity and righteousness; of honor, of truthfulness, love, patience, peace, kindness, goodness, and more. All these things come to us as fruits of our faith.

Holiness. People don't think about being holy very often.
Sanctification, or holiness, however, is our ultimate goal, and God's purpose for us in Jesus. "As He died to make men holy, let us die to make men free," from "The Battle Hymn of the Republic," is a wonderfully inspiring line. God is holy. God wants us to be with Him in eternity, but our sinfulness prevents us. So God Himself provided the way to holiness: His Son, who died for our sins, making us right with God, or justified, when we accept Christ's sacrifice for us, believe in His redeeming grace, and follow His Way. Godliness, holiness, the fruits of faith. But John Wesley, the founder of Methodism, believed that "the gospel of Christ knows of no

religion, but social; no holiness but social holiness." The point is that it is just not true faith or holiness if it is happening in isolation or in a vacuum. We are to do more than love God; we must also love our neighbors. We need to work together as disciples to nurture one another in grace. To cherish the grace of God at work in my own life, feeling wonderfully inspired, while I neglect my relationships with others is a vain sort of self-righteousness and can encroach on narcissism. True holiness or godliness relates to the holiness and godliness in others. Only together can we grow in purity. "Iron sharpens iron, one person sharpens the wits of another" (Proverbs 27:17).

Perfection. We may not be perfected in this lifetime, not in our fallen mortal posture. But we are to strive for perfection. Jesus tells us, "Be perfect, therefore, as your heavenly Father is perfect" (Matthew 5:48).

Strive for perfection. Press on. "I want to know Christ and the power of his resurrection and the sharing of his sufferings by becoming like him in his death, if somehow, I may attain the resurrection from the dead. Not that I have already obtained this, or have already reached the goal, but I press on to make it my own, because Christ Jesus has made me His own. Beloved, I do not consider that I have made it my own; but this one thing I do: Forgetting what lies behind and straining toward what lies ahead, I press on toward the goal for the prize of the heavenly call of God in Christ Jesus" (Philippians 3:10-14).

Think about these things. Concentrate. Give them your attention. Don't give up because it's hard to be pure, godly, or holy. Everything is hard at first. Focus your mind on the practice of purity and it will, in time, become natural to practice it. And once the practice of purity is part of your walk, you will be all the more able to experience the power of the kingdom in your life. It will work in you. You will belong to it. You will not be cast aside as one who is separated out like the fish in the parable of the dragnet. You will be gathered with the good.

To inspire you to think about whatever is pure, study what is in the scriptures:

The parable of the dragnet: "The kingdom of heaven is like a net that was thrown into the sea and gathered fish of every kind; when it was full, they drew it ashore, sat down, and put the good into baskets, but threw out the bad. So it will be at the end of the age. The angels will come out and separate the evil from the righteous, and throw them into the furnace of fire, where there will be weeping and gnashing of teeth" (Matthew 13: 47-50).

"You must understand this, that in the last days distressing times will come. For people will be lovers of themselves, lovers of money, boasters, arrogant, abusive, disobedient to their parents, ungrateful, unholy, inhuman, implacable, slanderers, profligates, brutes, haters of good, treacherous, reckless, swollen with conceit, lovers of pleasure rather than lovers of God, holding to the outward form of godliness but denying its power. Avoid them" (2 Timothy 3:1-5).

"All have sinned and fall short of the glory of God" (Romans 3:23).

"Shun fornication! Every sin that a person commits is outside the body, but the fornicator sins against the body itself" (1 Corinthians 6:18).

"Since we have these promises, beloved, let us cleanse ourselves from every defilement of body and of spirit, making holiness perfect in the fear of God" (2 Corinthians 7:1).

"This is the will of God, your sanctification: that you should abstain from fornication; that each of you know how to control your own body in holiness and honor, not with lustful passion, like the Gentiles who do not know God; that no one wrong or exploit a brother or sister in this matter, because the Lord is the avenger in all these things, just as we have already told you beforehand and solemnly warned you. For God did not call us to impurity, but in holiness. Therefore whoever rejects this does not reject human authority but God, who also gives His Holy Spirit to you" (1 Thessalonians 4:3-8).

"Abstain from every form of evil" (1 Thessalonians 5:22).
"May your spirit and soul and body be kept sound and blameless at the coming of our Lord Jesus Christ" (1 Thessalonians 5:23b).

"Put to death, therefore, whatever in you is earthly: fornication, impurity, passion, evil desire and greed (which is idolatry)" (Colossians 3:5)

"Let marriage be held in honor by all, and let the marriage bed kept undefiled; for God will judge fornicators and adulterers" (Hebrews 13:4).

"Religion that is pure and undefiled before God the Father is this: to care for orphans and widows in their distress and to keep oneself unstained by the world" (James 1:27).

"Draw near to God and He will draw near to you. Cleanse your hands, you sinners; and purify your hearts you double-minded" (James 4:8).

"Let no one despise your youth, but set the believers an example in speech and conduct, in love, in faith, in purity" (1 Timothy 4:12).

"How can young people keep their way pure? By guarding it according to your word" (Psalm 119:9).

"Who shall ascend the hill of the LORD? And who shall stand in his holy place? Those who have clean hands and pure hearts, who do not lift up their souls to what is false, and do not swear deceitfully" (Psalm 24:3-4).

"This is the covenant that I will make with the house of Israel after those days,' says the LORD, 'I will put my law within, and I will write it on their hearts; and I will be their God, and they shall be my people. No longer shall they teach one another, or say to each other, "Know the LORD," for they shall all know me, from the least of them to the greatest,' says the LORD. 'For I will forgive their iniquity, and remember their sin no more'" (Jeremiah 31:33-34).

"I will take you from the nations, and gather you from all the countries, and bring you into your own land. I will sprinkle clean water on you, and you will be clean from all your uncleanliness, and from all your idols I will cleanse you. A new heart I will give you, and a new spirit I will put within you" (Ezekiel 36:24-26).

"This is my prayer: that your love may overflow more and more with knowledge and full insight, to help you determine what is best, so that in the day of Christ you may be pure and blameless, having produced the harvest of righteousness that comes through Jesus Christ for the glory and praise of God" (Philippians 1:9-11).

"The LORD does not see as mortals see; they look on the outward appearance, but the LORD looks on the heart"(1 Samuel 16:7).

"The eye is the lamp of the body. So if your eye is healthy, your whole body will be full of light; but if your eyes are unhealthy, your whole body will be full of darkness. If then the light in you is darkness, how great is the darkness" (Matthew 6:22-23).

"Woe to you, scribes and Pharisees, hypocrites! For you clean the outside of the cup and of the plate, but inside they are full of greed and self-indulgence. You blind Pharisee! First clean the inside of the cup, so that the outside also may become clean as well. Woe to you, scribes and Pharisees, hypocrites! For you are like whitewashed tombs, which on the outside look beautiful, but on the inside they are full of the bones of the dead and of all kinds of filth" (Matthew 23:25-27).

"Let the wicked forsake their way, and the unrighteous their thoughts: and let him return to the LORD, that he may have mercy on them; and to our God, for he will abundantly pardon. For my thoughts are not your thoughts, nor are your ways my ways, says the LORD" (Isaiah 55:7-8).

"You must no longer live as the Gentiles live, in the futility of their minds. They are darkened in their understanding, alienated from the life of God because of their ignorance and hardness of heart. They have lost all sensitivity and have abandoned themselves to licentiousness, greedy to practice every kind of impurity. That is not the way you learned Christ. For surely you have heard about Him, as truth is in Jesus. You were taught to put away your former way of life, your old self, corrupt and deluded by its lusts, and to be renewed in the spirit of your minds; and to clothe yourselves with the new self, created according to the likeness of God in true righteousness and holiness" (Ephesians 4:17- 24).

"For it is the God, who said, 'Let light shine out of darkness,' who has shone in our hearts to give us the light of the knowledge of the glory of God in the face of Jesus Christ. But we have this treasure in clay jars, so that it may be made clear that this extraordinary power belongs to God and does not come from us"(2 Corinthians 4:6-7).

"Do you not know that your body is a temple of the Holy Spirit within you, which you have from God, and that you are not your own? For you were bought at a price. Therefore glorify God in your bodies" (1 Corinthians 6:19-20).

Stories

Purified water: Water can be made pure by boiling it, or by filtering it through several phases of minerals that remove impurities. One pastor once said, humorously, that to make holy water, you just boil the out of it.

After Adam and Eve ate the fruit from the tree of the knowledge of good and evil, and God questioned them, they began the blame game. Adam blamed Eve, and Eve blamed the serpent (Genesis 3:12- 13). The result of their sin was the Fall of humankind. And to this day, we live in a fallen world. We are defiled and in need of purification

"Put on the whole armor of God, so that you can take your stand against the wiles of the devil. For our struggle is not against enemies of blood and flesh, but against the rulers, against the authorities, against the cosmic powers of this present darkness, against the spiritual forces of evil in the heavenly places. Therefore take up the whole armor of God, so that you may be able to withstand on that evil day, and having done everything, to stand firm. Stand therefore, and fasten the belt of truth around your waist, and put on the breastplate of righteousness. As shoes for your feet put on whatever will make you ready to proclaim the gospel of peace. With all these, take the shield of faith, with which you will be able to quench all the flaming arrows of the evil one. Take the helmet of salvation, and the sword of the Spirit, which is the word of God" (Ephesians 6:10-18).

Gold is purified by fire. The ore is held over the fire in a crucible until it melts. The impurities rise to the surface and are scraped away until the refiner can see his reflection in the liquid gold. This process is repeated until the refiner is satisfied that the gold is pure. Only then is it poured into a mold and cooled. We are refined, as well, by the fires of our trials as well as by the fires of the practice of purity.

"The kingdom of heaven is like treasure hidden in a field, which someone found and hid; then in his joy he goes and sells all he has and buys that field. Again, the kingdom of heaven is like a merchant in search of fine pearls; on finding one pearl of great value, he went and sold everything he had and bought it" (Matthew 13:44- 46). My prayer is that your treasure will be discovered undefiled and that the beauty of your pearls will be an inspiration.

My older brother and I each received a nickel for some backyard chore and were on our way to the drugstore a few blocks away to buy packs of baseball cards (which cost five cents each back then). To get there, we walked down a cinder drive behind the Winnetka Community House. We were talking about the cards we hoped we'd receive, and how Robert would give me any doubles he got, since I was only beginning to collect baseball cards, when I spotted a coin in the cinders. Excitedly, I picked up a very beat-up old quarter. Many feet, cars, and trucks must have traveled over it throughout time, scratching it and wearing it dark and almost impossible to discern. My brother suggested that it was probably no good anymore, at least, not worth five nickels. When we got to the store, I went directly to the counter and asked the man if this old quarter was any good. He said, "Yes, son. It's still worth twenty-five cents." I lit up and bought five packs (I now had thirty cents, but I had to pay tax), and I gave Robert the doubles I got that day. Even though that quarter was defiled and dirty, it was still worth its original value. Likewise my soul and yours.

Clean water. Some of the effects of drinking contaminated water can be immediate. These include gastrointestinal and stomach illnesses like nausea, vomiting, cramps, and diarrhea. Cholera can spread, and people can die from impure water. Bacteria, herbicides, and pesticides can seep into the water supply. Even lead from old plumbing pipes can be a serious problem. Pure water is essential for survival of many lifeforms. We need uncontaminated water.

Soren Kierkegaard wrote a wonderful treatise entitled *Purity of Heart Is to Will One Thing*. Check it out; he believes purity of heart is holiness.

What to Do

Repent. "All have sinned and fall short of the glory of God" (Romans 3:23). The good news is that "they are now justified by his grace as a gift, through the redemption that is in Christ Jesus" (Romans 3:24).

Confess. "If we say we have no sin, we deceive ourselves, and the truth is not in us .If we confess our sins, he who is faithful and just will forgive us our sins and cleanse us from all unrighteousness" (1 John 1:8- 9).

Forgive and be forgiven. "Forgive us our debts, as we also have forgiven our debtors.... For if you forgive others their trespasses, your heavenly Father will also forgive you. But if you do not forgive others, neither will your Father forgive your trespasses" (Matthew 6:12, 14).

If you are dating, boys, remember that that girl you like will someday be someone's wife; girls, remember that that boy you like will someday be someone's husband.

Don't feed your passion. It is normal to think sexual thoughts at times, but to feed them with fantasies can be unhealthy. Though our culture may believe in such a thing as a healthy fantasy life, we can become all too easily tempted. Take to heart this truth from the letter of James: "One is tempted by one's own desire, being lured and enticed by it; then, when that desire has conceived, it gives birth to sin; and that sin, when it is full-grown, gives birth to death" (James 1:14- 15). I love the quote from Kahlil Gibran: "If your heart is a volcano, how shall you expect flowers to bloom in your hands?" "Can fire be carried in the bosom, without burning one's clothes?" (Proverbs 6:27).

Purify your bodies. Do not eat or drink anything that is bad for you. That includes sugary foods and alcohol. Drink fresh or pure water. It has a cleansing effect. I have had five episodes of kidney stones, and I don't like that pain. I try to avoid it by drinking lots of water every day. Of course, don't smoke. I've seen many people with lung diseases suffer terribly at the end of their lives, unable to breathe. The poison of recreational drugs that bring a false high is bad for your brain. Think about whatever is pure, and you will develop an attitude and actions (practice) that will help you live longer.

Be an advocate for clean water. Help to build wells where they are needed, especially in poor areas of the world that need new wells so desperately.

Be thankful l if your tap water has been properly treated in your city or town. Be conscious of your water systems. Be grateful for the sanitation and waste systems where you live. Don't regret your water, garbage, or sewage bills. They support cleanliness. Likewise, be grateful for other public works systems where you live; street cleaning comes from such sources. And be glad you can shower, bathe, wash your dishes, and clean your clothes. Imagine what life would be like without water. And celebrate the blessings.

Acknowledge purity as you experience it in forms of entertainment, such as movies and TV shows. There is nothing like some good, clean fun. Keep it clean.

Be responsible for the purity in your life and surroundings. Others may tell dirty jokes or use vulgar language, but you don't have to, and you can call others to clean up their act. What does faith in Christ compel you to do?

A Song
I love the Lord with the heart of my heart
and the whole of my soul,
and the music that's started to come
lets me know I can smile.
And I'm happy to stop for a while
and look into heaven and pray.
And I love the Lord with the words of my song
and the music I play, and the fire of my longing.
It's started to stay in my eyes.
And it's warmer than yesterday's skies,
where the sunshine seemed farther away.
Yes, I love the Lord for the way that He cares

and the smile that He gives as He answers my prayers.

A Prayer
0 Lord, I want to be more holy in my heart and in my life, in my thoughts and in my actions. Purify my will. Let love and integrity envelop me until my faith is perfected and my desires are no longer in conflict with Your Spirit. In Jesus's great name, I pray. Amen

CHAPTER FIVE

Whatever is Pleasing

> How lovely is your dwelling place, 0 LORD of hosts!
> My soul longs, indeed it faints, for the courts of the LORD;
> my heart and my flesh sing for joy to the living God.
> PSALM 84:1-2

The word *pleasing* is also translated "lovely" in the New International Version. For this chapter, I will consider what is lovely. Of course, anything lovely is also pleasing.

I can remember a day a long time ago that made the word lovely stand out forever in my mind. It was the summer I turned eighteen. I was walking over to a friend's house about a mile away, and I came upon a woman, about fifty years old, who was carrying two bags of groceries. She had gotten herself about two and a half blocks away from the store, and she was beginning to find that she shouldn't have made this trip on foot. The bags were getting very awkward and heavy (they didn't have the plastic bags with handles yet). From about two blocks behind her, I saw her stop and hoist first one bag to get a better grip on it and then the other.

I guessed that even though she may not have had a long way to go, I could be a good Boy Scout and offer to carry her groceries for her. So I ran up behind her and asked if I could help out. She was so grateful and relieved to know that I would do that for her; she said, "That would be lovely." She gave me one bag and was going to carry the other herself until I insisted on carrying both; she looked like she needed a break.

I asked her how much farther she had to go, and she told me her address on Vernon Lane, sounding like she hoped it wouldn't take me too far out of my way. Coincidently, it just so happened that she lived on the same street as the girl I was going to see. And when I told her I was going to the home of Sue McCartney, she sounded like she'd hit the jackpot when she said that she lived right next door.

Well, we walked for about four more blocks together, and she seemed very interested in knowing what Sue and I were going to be doing that afternoon, and what sort of things we'd done together at the beach where we had met, saying, "How lovely!" about everything I told her.

When I dropped off the bags of groceries and turned to leave, I said, "Have a nice day, now."
She said, "It's a lovely day," and then she said to tell Sue that she had a wonderful boyfriend. You know, she really made my day. She made it lovely. And though the relationship with Sue didn't last (my best friend, Jack, liked her too, and since I had other girlfriends and he didn't have any, I led her to him), she and I had a lovely afternoon that day.

Think of the natural beauty that surrounds you. A sunset can be lovely, a forest path, a pleasant shoreline, a mountaintop, a canyon. These things are so lovely, they can be inspiring. And many things that are inspiring are lovely. I am inspired by my wife's positive attitude and enjoyment of the scriptures while she endures the limitations of the disease of multiple sclerosis in her body. It is inspirational to hear about the overcoming of an injury or disease followed by the accomplishment of great physical actions, like the paralyzed young girl who eventually becomes able to dance beautifully, or the star athlete who forgoes great fortune in order to focus on the needs of a daughter who is ill. These inspirational stories are pleasing to hear about. Lovely.

What is it that makes something lovely? You hear the word used often at the end of a date: "I had a lovely time." It's used to describe the way someone is dressed: "You look lovely." Or "Isn't she lovely?" And in many respects, it is those things that are beautiful or gorgeous that evoke that word from us, especially as we describe their inspirational qualities.

That's what makes something lovely: its inspirational quality. Something that is lovely and inspirational touches a nerve within us and generates admiration. Whatever is lovely is so pleasing and special that we want to cherish it, to hold it close, to express a reverence for it, to search for it the way a merchant searches for fine pearls. We search for those things that are so delightful, so exquisite, so extraordinary that they are not only pleasing but charming, enchanting, exceptional, and adorable. These are things that are lovely. They are like the kingdom of heaven (Matthew 13:45-46).

But the loveliness is not just in those pearls. The loveliness is in what they can mean. The loveliness is within us when we call them lovely. That loveliness may be inspired by those pearls, but the quality of what makes them so precious is the way they make us feel. They can be profoundly remarkable. They can be astounding. They can bring a tear to your eye.

The word *lovely* is a word that describes something. And it describes it as being of love. Something that is lovely is of love. A lovely deed is done out of love. To describe a night out as a lovely evening is to imply that it was full of love. To say it's a lovely day is to suggest it's a day full of love. To say that someone looks lovely is to state that they fill our hearts with love. And to proclaim that a present is lovely is to claim it as a gift of love.

Think about the things in your life that are so special to you that you cherish them. Or the experiences that you cherish in your heart. Look at some pictures you have taken. What is it that makes them so special? Is it connected with a person who is special or an occasion that became special to you? Is it something inspiring because of some unique quality that gives it an intrinsic value? And if you were able to share that special thing that you adore so much, would you be able to transmit the value it has, its inspirational qualities? If so, lovely.

Lovely. Are you like the merchant in the parable of Christ? Are you in search of something lovely? How will you find it? Can you be someone who is lovely? Do you try to do things that are lovely, pleasing, inspiring? Where do you think you might find the pearl of greatest value? Is it in the church? The church you attend can be a lovely place, a place of inspiration. Do you help to make it that way? "One thing I asked of the Lord, that will I seek after: to live in the house of the Lord all the days of my life, to behold the beauty of the Lord, and to inquire in His temple" (Psalm 27:4).

What, to you, is the pearl of greatest price? What would you do to find it, to possess it? What would you give up for the sake of the preciousness of the kingdom of heaven? This kingdom is so completely inspirational that all people want to experience it, because it is full other glory of God. Its radiance is like a most rare jewel. Its gates are made of something so special you couldn't help but feel welcome there; you couldn't help but feel lovely as you passed through them. To feel the inspiration of heaven is to feel something divine. What is lovely is divine. It sets your heart on fire with its power. What is it that has this power in your life? What are the things that are lovely? Think about these things. Meditate on them day and night. Share them. Give them as gifts. Receive the gifts you are given with the knowledge that they are lovely gifts; they are gifts of love.

To inspire you to think about whatever is lovely, inspiring, and pleasing, study what is in the scriptures:

"He has made everything beautiful in its time. He has also set eternity in the human heart; yet no one can fathom what God has done from beginning to end" (Ecclesiastes 3:11 NIV).

"His delight is not in the strength of the horse, nor his pleasure in the legs of the runner; but the Lord takes pleasure in those who fear him, who put their hope in his unfailing love" (Psalm 14 7:10-11).

Try to find out what is pleasing to the Lord" (Ephesians 5:10).

"We also have as our ambition, whether at home or absent, to be pleasing to Him" (2 Corinthians 5:9).

"Children, obey to your parents in all things, for this is well-pleasing to the Lord" (Colossians 3:20 NKJV).

"Am I now seeking human approval, or God's approval? Or am I trying to please people? If I were still pleasing people, I would not be a servant of Christ" (Galatians 1:10).

"Just as we have been approved by God to be entrusted with the message of the gospel, even so we speak, not to please mortals, but to please God who tests our hearts" (1 Thessalonians 2:4).

"The Lord takes pleasure in His people; He adorns the humble with victory" (Psalm 149:4).

"Those of blameless ways are His delight" (Proverbs 11:20). "Those who are in the flesh cannot please God" (Romans 8:8). "Without faith it is impossible to please Him" (Hebrews 11:6).

"Not everyone who says to Me, 'Lord, Lord,' will enter the kingdom of heaven, but only the one who does the will of My Father in heaven" (Matthew 7:21).

"From childhood you have known the sacred writings which are able to give you the wisdom that leads to salvation through faith which is in Christ Jesus. All Scripture is inspired by God and is profitable for teaching, for reproof, for correction, for training in righteousness; that the man of God may be adequate, equipped for every good work" (2 Timothy 3:15-17 NASB).

"How beautiful [also *lovely*] on the mountains are the feet of the messenger who announces peace, who brings good news, who announces salvation, who says to Zion, 'Your God reigns'" (Isaiah 52:7).

Stories

"The kingdom of heaven is like treasure hidden in a field, which someone found and hid, and then in his joy goes and sells all he has and buys that field. Again, the kingdom of heaven is like a merchant in search of fine pearls; on finding one pearl of great value, he went and sold all that he had and bought it" (Matthew 13:44-46).

"One of the seven angels who had the seven bowls full of the seven last plagues came and said to me, 'Come, I will show you the bride, the wife of the Lamb.' And in the Spirit he carried me away to a great high mountain, and showed me the Holy City, Jerusalem, coming down out of heaven from God. It has the glory of God, and a radiance like a very rare jewel, like a jasper, clear as crystal. It has a great, high wall with twelve gates, and at the gated twelve angels" (Revelation 21:9-12).

"The twelve gates are twelve pearls, each of the gates is a single pearl" (Revelation 21:21).

In kindergarten, I made a finger-painting that the teacher ooohed and ahhhed about. When I took it home, my mother ooohed and ahhhed about it. It went up on the family bulletin board. Later, I gave it to my Granny Lee (Leila), who mounted it in a frame and hung it on the wall just inside her front door. I guess it was a special piece of art I felt special because my art was so admired.

Rick Hoyt was born in 1962 to Dick and Judy Hoyt. As a result of oxygen deprivation to Rick's brain at the time of his birth, he was a quadriplegic with cerebral palsy. But in the spring of 1977, Rick told his father that he wanted to participate in a five-mile benefit run for a lacrosse player who had been paralyzed in an accident. Far from being a long-distance runner, Dick agreed to push Rick in his wheelchair, and they finished all five miles, coming in next to last. That night, Rick told his father, "Dad, when I'm running, it feels like I'm not handicapped." Dick retired in 1995 from the Air National Guard after serving his country for thirty-seven years. Over the years, Team Hoyt participated many times in races and special runs, logging thousands of miles. Seeing Dick pushing Rick along the roads in his special racing wheelchair was a wonderful inspiration.

What to do
Watch a sunrise or sunset. Lovely. Give thanks for the wonderful colors you see, and let the experience inspire you. Gifts of love from God.

Have you seen the aurora borealis, the northern lights? Or the southern lights? Awesome.

Look through a telescope. Let the stars evoke awe.

Look through a microscope. Even a single cell can give a sense of wonder.

Watch, or remember, how a child takes their first steps. It can bring a tear to your eye.

When your child becomes able to hit the ball, catch the ball, make a basket, do a somersault, or climb a tree, it can be inspiring.

My family loves to go on hikes in the woods at forest preserves, state parks, and national monuments. The beauty of nature, creeks bubbling, and sunshine through the leaves is glorious. The trees in autumn are so beautiful, you wish you could see them all the time. But there is even splendor in a single blade of grass. Or a tree:

> I think that I shall never see
> A poem lovely as a tree.
> - Joyce Kilmer

Read *Guideposts* for inspirational stories related to faith. Or find inspirational words, quotes, and readings on the Internet. Inspirational stories are all around you. Find them; meditate on them. Think about these things. Retell some of those stories to people who might be inspired by them.

Read the Bible. Paul wrote to Timothy that the Word of God is inspired. God's Spirit is literally breathed into it. Study the Bible. Join a Bible study, share how the words of scripture inspire you in your spiritual journey, and hear how it inspires others. I have known some people who return to the same recurring retreat or study the same chapter of scripture to recapture the experiences that have moved them.

Listen to or read sermons by a favorite preacher. Consider what may have inspired them to preach God's Word as they have.

Go on a Christian spiritual retreat or cursillo. They can offer great opportunities.

Look for the inspirational. Be an inspiration.

Checks and balances. Beware of constantly seeking emotional highs. The merchant in search of pearls might have starved to death if he didn't also search for a meal now and then. Never neglect your practical needs and your earthly purpose. I have known people who abandoned their nice, stable jobs in order to pursue a passion that could not earn them a living. It might be different with respect to a life of faith, but beware. We can get caught up in what Sarah Ban Breathnach, in her book, Simple Abundance, calls "emotional binging." As wonderful as it is to be caught up in a divine inspiration, never let yourself become so heavenly minded that you are no earthly good.

A Song

Sunset Skies

When I saw the evening sunset burning crimson as it colored cloudy skies,

I beheld the flowing beauty of the freedom when a bird takes off and flies.
As I sat before a forest in a clearing of a splendid color green, there became a lovely vision of a gentle, tender woman to be seen.

Well, I loved her when I saw her,
and I soon began to know her every thought.
And I was always grateful
for the joy of every pleasure that she brought.
She was lovely, she was lonely,
she was gentle, she was tender, she was kind.
And I loved her as the only
kind of woman that could ever ease my mind.

When I brought her close beside me, I could give her all my loving all the time.
And I felt a very tender type of loving soon begin and start to climb.
When she met a lonely friend of mine who needed all her loving more than me,
I could see there was no keeping me from letting come the love that ought to be.

Well, he loved her when he saw her,
and he soon began to know her every thought.
And he was always grateful
for the joy of every pleasure that she brought.
She was lovely, they were lonely,
she was gentle, she was tender, she was kind.
And he knew her as the only
kind of woman that could ever ease his mind.

When I saw the evening sunset burning crimson as it colored cloudy skies,
I beheld the flowing beauty of the freedom as a bird takes off and flies.
I had found a lovely woman who could seem to make her lover always smile.

But I was not as lonely, and I'm proud to say that she was mine awhile.

Now if you look at me more closely, you can see I've got a freedom in my eyes.

And that freedom there can come to me just looking at the sunset in the skies.

A Prayer

Almighty God, You have given us eyes to see the pleasing sights of creation; ears to hear the joyful sounds of birds and brooks, of winds and waves; and the sense of touch to feel the breeze and the warmth of the sun. Thank You. May the gifts of all our senses awaken in us the inspiration of Your grace at work all around us and within. May the pleasing things of this life likewise remind us of how blessed we truly are, and may our response be seen in the ways we want to not only cherish the wonder but pass it on to others. May we become a part of all that is good and lovely and full of grace. This I ask in Jesus's name. Amen.

CHAPTER SIX

Whatever is Gracious

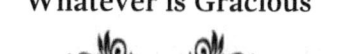

> If anyone forces you to go one mile, go also the second mile.
> MATTHEW 5:41

Many people do gracious things, even though they may not know it, even though they might not call it gracious. It might just be considered something friendly. But to do something gracious is to do something not called for, going out of the way to show a kindness or to care. Showing hospitality, taking a neighbor a surprise plate of cookies, shoveling snow from their sidewalk, inviting them to worship with you: These all are simple examples of graciousness. Some congregations even have hospitality teams that make sure everyone (not just visitors) always feel welcomed. It is a gracious thing when the new resident is welcomed to the neighborhood by all the neighbors. It is a gracious thing when a dish is brought to a family after a loved one dies. It was a gracious thing when the Good Samaritan helped the man beaten by robbers and left for dead on the road to Jericho. But graciousness and kindness go hand in hand. And those things that are gracious are generally unexpected, quite extraordinary, and touching.

Many years ago in Nigeria, there was an epidemic of smallpox. At a church mission hospital, in order to protect those already admitted for care, the sick people who came in were examined carefully to determine whether there were any early symptoms of the disease. There was a woman who came, weak and weary, and ready to give birth. But after she was examined, several signs of smallpox were found on her body. She needed to be cared for in isolation.

The staff doctor asked among the midwives for a volunteer. A long pause was ended by a woman named Matilda, who offered her assistance, knowing the risks. Soon the baby was born, a little boy. Thankfully, he had not been affected by the mother's disease. But his mother became worse, and after a few more days, she died.

Some of the Christians at the hospital thought that since Matilda had put her own fears aside to aid the mother in her final days, God would protect her from the smallpox. But soon, the spots appeared, and Matilda came down with a serious case of the disease. For a week, it seemed as though she wouldn't make it. But she did recover, and she continued to serve at the risk of her own health.

I tell this story because Matilda was gracious.

Early in his public service in South Africa, Mohandas Gandhi led a protest against the English mandate that claimed that any marriage other than a Christian marriage was not legal. This, he said, made their children illegitimate and their wives and them immoral. Not only that, but any non-white people were compelled to carry a pass that police could demand to see at any time. Should they not have their pass, they could be arrested. In a protest, Gandhi began burning these passes, a symbol of the inequality and injustice surrounding the people of South Africa. He burned them one by one. The police present used clubs to deter him, but he persisted, not by fighting back at the police but by continuing to burn passes, even though beaten to the ground and broken.

A few days later, at a meeting of colored people, many of whom were severely angry and willing to fight, Gandhi said that their courage was good, and that, yes, they all had a cause for which they were prepared to die, but he told them there was no cause for which he was willing to kill. He would attack no one, kill no one. He wanted the people to fight against the anger of the whites in power, not to provoke it. He would not return evil for evil.

Gandhi was a gracious man. And he lived by the principles of non-violent resistance that were inspired in part by Christ's words about turning the other cheek.

In fact, it is the Christian way that goes beyond just turning the other cheek. Because the Christian way is to return evil with good. Going out of your way to show a better way. If someone takes your coat, give them your cloak as well. If someone forces you to go one mile under their burden, show them your graciousness by going even farther than they expect (Matthew 5:39-41).

There is a more recent story of a young South African black man named Robert. As he watched a group of white men attack and kill his father, he swore he would never forget their faces. He grew into adulthood with a bitter attitude toward all white people, but his faith kept him from letting his anger get the better of him, and he even tried to urge his friends not to fight injustice with anger. Many years after he watched his father die, he saw another group of white men attack the home of a poor black family. This time, though, the whites didn't know what was in store for them. Soon, they found themselves surrounded. A bloody fight ensued. One white man was left for dead near a clump of bushes at the side of a hill. As Robert came close, he heard him moan. Having pity on him, he came to his side. He was shocked when he looked closely at the man's bloody face. It was one of the men who had beaten his father.

At first, he felt a flash of anger and was tempted to push the man down the embankment to his death. But the desire to end the man's life turned to pity. He bandaged the man's wounds and gave him water and care, until he could return to his white friends.

"You could have killed me," he said to Robert. "Why didn't you?"
"Because you killed my father," said Robert.

After that, the white man began to tell his friends that the killing had to stop. He felt as though it already had.

Another story about graciousness.

Graciousness is something that happens all the time. Ruth was gracious to Naomi. Ruth was gracious in her gleaning, working where she wasn't asked to work, doing good where it was not expected. And in return, Boaz was gracious to Ruth, opening the door for her, accepting her, and being especially kind to her.

Graciousness is going above and beyond the call of duty. What is the duty of a Christian? Matilda risked her life for the sake of another. Gandhi risked his for the sake of principles of justice and equality. In a world where retaliation would be expected when provocation occurs, the Christian is called to rise above anger and resentment. In a culture where we feel as though it is a right to strike back at the other guy because "he hit me first"- the old "eye for an eye" mentality- we are called to fight against sin; fight not against a person physically, but morally; fighting not out of anger, but out of love. We are compelled to be gracious.

We are saved by faith, not by violence. We are faithful by grace, and by faith we are gracious.

Christ would have us love our enemies in order to change them. Fighting them and killing them doesn't change the person, but it can make you a sinner. It may change some of the circumstances by eliminating a few problem individuals, but it doesn't solve the problem. Paul even said, in Romans 12:20, "If your enemies are hungry, feed them; if they are thirsty, give them something to drink; for by doing this you will heap burning coals upon their heads." To fight back with kindness is to make the enemy feel ashamed by meeting their evil with good. That shame becomes anguish equal to the anguish of the burning coals. Paul says, "Do not be overcome by evil, but overcome evil with good" (Romans 12:21).

How far should we let the evil go, though? How provoked shall we allow ourselves to be?

An aside, here. I am far enough from perfect that I need to confess my very human unwillingness to go the whole distance here. I am trying, but I fall short because should I see someone about to harm my wife, my children, or grandchildren, I would do all I could to prevent them. I would become a raving madman, even at the risk of losing my own soul. Perhaps it is paternal instinct or love that would compel me, but I know, with Gandhi, I am truly not willing to kill. I do want to relinquish an evil person or group of their power, however.

But Jesus said, "Do not resist an evildoer" (Matthew 5:39). I think Jesus Himself becomes the answer. He let Himself be crucified. He denied Himself completely, and He even prayed from the Cross, "Father, forgive them; for they do not know what they are doing" (Luke 23:34).

There, then, is the vision of what we must think and how we must act. It is a vision of giving even our lives in order to show graciousness. But there are different ways of giving our lives than by letting ourselves be trampled underfoot or being beaten to death or tortured without resisting.

Begin with the belief, the understanding that someone else's soul is more important than your earthly life. Realize that Jesus Christ died for their sins too. You can see them as forgiven sinners, even though they may not have yet discovered that redeeming grace. You, and the way you act so graciously, may be the one who begins to set them free, as you see in the story of Robert in South Africa. You may be the one God is working through to bring a little light into their darkness. It may take risking your own well-being at times; it may even force you to go out of your way a bit, but we, as Christians, are not followers of our own way or of the world's way. We are followers of Jesus Christ.

The heritage of an Israelite is the heritage of a Christian. In Deuteronomy 15: 7-11, there is a prescription for graciousness. Realize that the needy may be those who have been surrounded by great darkness and are in desperate need of light. And realize that the poor may also be those who are morally bankrupt. Open your hand. It may get bitten, but at least be willing to take that risk. Be willing to go out on a limb once in a while. To be a Christian is to be willing to serve above and beyond the call of duty.

How far did Jesus go to bring you grace?
We can be gracious because we have been given grace.

To inspire you to think about whatever is gracious, kind, favorable, and hospitable, as well as inspiring, study what is in the scriptures:

"If anyone is poor among your fellow Israelites in any of the towns of the land the LORD your God is giving you, do not be hardhearted or tightfisted toward them. Rather, be openhanded and freely lend them whatever they need.... Give generously to them and do so without a grudging heart; then because of this the LORD your God will bless you in all your work and in everything you put your hand to. There will always be poor people in the land. Therefore I command you to be openhanded toward your fellow Israelites who are poor and needy in your land" (Deuteronomy 15:7-8, 10-11 NIV).

"Let your graciousness be known to everyone. The Lord is near"(Philippians 4:5 HCSB).

"Whoever finds me finds life and obtains favor from the Lord" (Proverbs 8:35).

"Do not be afraid, Mary; for you have found favor with God" (Luke 1:30).

"Jesus increased in wisdom and in years, and in divine and human favor" (Luke 2:52).

"May the LORD make His face shine on you, and be gracious to you" (Numbers 6:25).

"The LORD waits to be gracious to you; therefore He will rise up to show mercy to you. For the LORD is a God of justice; blessed are all those who wait for Him" (Isaiah 30:18).

"Be kind to one another, tender-hearted, forgiving one another, as God in Christ has forgiven you" (Ephesians 4:32).

"Do not neglect to show hospitality to strangers, for by doing that some have entertained angels without knowing it" (Hebrews 13:2).

"The LORD appeared to Abraham by the oaks of Mamre as he sat at the entrance of his tent in the heat of the day. He looked up and saw three men standing near him. When he saw them, he ran from the tent entrance to meet them and bowed down to the ground. He said, 'My Lord, if I have found favor with you, do not pass by your servant. Let a little water be brought, and wash your feet, and rest yourselves under this tree. Let me bring a little bread, that may refresh yourselves, and after that you may pass on-since you have come to your servant'" (Genesis 18:1-5).

"As He sat at dinner in the house, many tax collectors and sinners came and were sitting with Him and His disciples. When the Pharisees saw this, they said to his disciples, 'Why does your teacher eat with tax collectors and sinners?' But when He heard this, He said, 'Those who are well have no need of a physician, but those who are sick. Go and learn what this means: "I desire mercy, not sacrifice." For I have come not to call the righteous, but sinners'" (Matthew 9:10-12).

Jesus was gracious enough to enter Matthew's home, but notice the lack of grace among the Pharisees:

"When one of the Pharisees invited Jesus to have dinner with him, he went to the Pharisee's house and reclined at the table. A woman in that town who lived a sinful life learned that Jesus was eating at the Pharisee's house, so she came there with an alabaster jar of perfume. As she stood behind him at his feet weeping, she began to wet his feet with her tears. Then she wiped them with her hair, kissed them and poured perfume on them. When the Pharisee who had invited him saw this, he said to himself, 'If this man were a prophet, he would know who is touching him and what kind of woman she is-that she is a sinner.' Jesus answered him, 'Simon, I have something to tell you.' 'Tell me, teacher,' he said. 'Two people owed money to a certain moneylender. One owed him five hundred denarii, and the other fifty. Neither of them had the money to pay him back, so he forgave the debts of both. Now which of them will love him more?' Simon replied, 'I suppose the one who had the bigger debt forgiven.' 'You have judged correctly,' Jesus said. Then he turned toward the woman and said to Simon, 'Do you see this woman? I came into your house. You did not give me any water for my feet, but she wet my feet with her tears and wiped them with her hair. You did not give me a kiss, but this woman, from the time I entered, has not stopped kissing my feet. You did not put oil on my head, but she has poured perfume on my feet. Therefore, I tell you, her many sins have been forgiven-as her great love has shown. But whoever has been forgiven little loves little.' Then Jesus said to her, 'Your sins are forgiven'" (Luke 7: 36-48 NIV).

Though it was gracious of the man to invite Jesus into his home, it was the woman who went out of her way to be gracious to Jesus, and then Jesus became very gracious to her.

Stories

I like the movie *Forrest Gump*. It's about a boy who was mildly developmentally delayed and the man he becomes. In one of the early scenes, Forrest gets on the school bus. As he walks down the aisle looking for a place to sit, boy after boy tells him, "This seat's taken." Finally, a girl named Jenny tells him, "You can sit here." She welcomes him. Her kindness was gracious.

Because I am a United Methodist pastor, our family has moved several times, going wherever we were sent. Often meals, cookies, pies, and treats have been brought to our door by neighbors or welcoming members of the new congregation I was serving (sometimes, even on the day we moved in). On one occasion, after several weeks, my congregation had what they called a "pound shower." The idea is to stock the family's pantry with several pounds of food. It was a wonderful sign of hospitality. How gracious that was.

Another time, on the day we moved in, after everything was taken off the truck, a wonderful woman, an older member of the church named Rose, came by, introduced herself, and said, "I'm here to make all your beds." It was a perfect gift. We located the boxes with our linens and sorted the sheets to their various beds, and she began her task. It was just the right task for this nice lady and so good of her to do, because by the time we would have gotten around to making the beds, we wouldn't have wanted to do one more thing. How gracious.

Ananias was convinced by the Holy Spirit to be gracious to Paul after he was blinded on the road to Damascus: "Now there was a disciple at Damascus named Ananias. The Lord said to him in a vision, 'Ananias.' And he said, 'Here I am, Lord.' And the Lord said to him, 'Rise and go to the street called Straight, and at the house of Judas look for a man of Tarsus named Saul, for behold, he is praying, and he has seen in a vision a man named Ananias come in and lay his hands on him so that he might regain his sight.' But Ananias answered, 'Lord, I have heard from many about this man, how much evil he has done to your saints at Jerusalem. And here he has authority from the chief priests to bind all who call on your name.' But the Lord said to him, 'Go, for he is a chosen instrument of mine to carry my name before the Gentiles and kings and the children of Israel. For I will show him how much he must suffer for the sake of my name.' So Ananias departed and entered the house. And laying his hands on him he said, 'Brother Saul, the Lord Jesus who appeared to you on the road by which you came has sent me so that you may regain your sight and be filled with the Holy Spirit.' And immediately something like scales fell from his eyes, and he regained his sight. Then he rose and was baptized; and taking food, he was strengthened" (Acts 9:10- 19 ESV).

Even Jesus had to be convinced to be gracious one time: "Jesus withdrew to the region of Tyre and Sidon. A Canaanite woman from that vicinity came to him, crying out, 'Lord, Son of David, have mercy on me! My daughter is demon-possessed and suffering terribly.' Jesus did not answer a word. So his disciples came to him and urged him, 'Send her away, for she keeps crying out after us.' He answered, 'I was sent only to the lost sheep of Israel.' The woman came and knelt before him. 'Lord, help me!' she said. He replied, 'It is not right to take the children's bread and toss it to the dogs.' 'Yes, it is, Lord,' she said. 'Even the dogs eat the crumbs that fall from their master's table.' Then Jesus said to her, 'Woman, you have great faith! Your request is granted.' And her daughter was healed at that moment" (Luke 15:21- 28 NIV).

Ruth graciously welcomed her daughters-in-law to come with her when she wanted to return to Israel. But she also graciously gave them permission to stay in Moab: "When Naomi heard in Moab that the Lord had come to the aid of his people by providing food for them, she and her daughters-in-law prepared to return home from there. With her two daughters-in-law she left the place where she had been living and set out on the road that would take them back to the land of Judah. Then Naomi said to her two daughters-in-law, 'Go back, each of you, to your mother's home. May the LORD show you kindness, as you have shown kindness to your dead husbands and to me? May the LORD grant that each of you will find rest in the home of another husband?' Then she kissed them goodbye and they wept aloud and said to her, 'We will go back with you to your people.' But Naomi said, 'Return home, my daughters. Why would you come with me?'" (Ruth 1:6-11 NIV).

Orpah returned, but Ruth very graciously stayed with Naomi: "Ruth replied, 'don't urge me to leave you or to turn back from you. Where you go I will go, and where you stay I will stay. Your people will be my people and your God my God. Where you die I will die, and there I will be buried. May the LORD deal with me, be it ever so severely, if even death separates you and me'" (Ruth 1:16- 17 NIV).

Soon, a man named Boaz, a kinsman of Naomi's from Bethlehem, was gracious to Ruth: "I've been told all about what you have done for your mother-in-law since the death of your husband-how you left your father and mother and your homeland and came to live with a people you did not know before. May the LORD repay you for what you have done. May you be richly rewarded by the LORD, the God of Israel, under whose wings you have come to take refuge" (Ruth 2:11-12 NIV).

What to Do

Be gracious. Go out of your way to be kind. It doesn't hurt, though it can be humbling.

Do not retaliate. We're not in the schoolyard any more. The Old Testament adage of "an eye for an eye" (Exodus 21:23-25) is not what Jesus taught.

Offer to do a favor for someone: rake their yard without asking to be paid; shovel the snow from their sidewalk, clean their house.

Show hospitality and welcome a stranger.

Churches may need a hospitality committee. Start one, or join one.

Some churches give gifts of various kinds to first-time attenders.

Visit a nursing home as a choir, sing to the people, and bring them cupcakes.

Visit a shut-in. Give them your time, such a generous and gracious gift.

Give to a cause that serves people who are less fortunate or who have come upon hard times: a clothing giveaway; a food pantry; a shelter for the homeless or abused. These places need volunteers and supplies.

Donate blood, or blood platelets, or plasma! I've been doing it for forty years, and the blood bank has given me gifts and put my name on a wall of fame. There can be rewards for our graciousness.

Be on the list for bone-marrow donations, or arrange to have your organs donated after you die.

Gifts can be given at any time but are especially welcome at Christmas.

Decorate the house of an elderly person who can't do it anymore.

Read to the blind or offer rides to people who can no longer get out on their own.
Help someone when they move in to their new home.

A Song

Shining Eyes

Come, let me tell you
  of how I can see today,
  and how I know now life cannot be the same.
Tell us, 0 shining eyes,
  who brought this healing touch?
  Where does He come from and what is His name?

First, let me tell you
  my birth came with blindness
  through no sin of others and no sin of mine.
Somehow, my sightless eyes
  were made for a purpose
  that's bringing to light some great glory divine.

Jesus of Nazareth,
 sent by His Father's love,
He is the sunrise that pierces the night. Jesus of Nazareth,
   filled with grace from above,
   He is the reason I walk in the light.

Now there's a freedom
   the world had been waiting for.
   Now there's a joy that will make us all whole.
Jesus my healer,
   my Lord, and my Savior,
   come and believe Him with all of your soul.
Jesus of Nazareth,
   sent by His Father's love,
   He is the sunrise that pierces the night.
Jesus of Nazareth,
   filled with grace from above,
   come and receive His new blessing of sight.

A Prayer
   Almighty and gracious God, help us to learn that we can be gracious toward others. Let us offer grace to others, not because of who they are, but because of who we are, and help us remember that we are people who have received grace upon grace. We ask this in Jesus's name. Amen.

CHAPTER SEVEN

If there is any excellence

Be perfect , therefore, as your heaven Father is perfect.
MATTHEW 5:48

"When the dog bites, when the beestings, when I'm feeling sad, I simply remember my favorite things, and then I don't feel so bad."

This is the refrain from the song "My Favorite Things" from The Sound of Mu sic. It reflects the idea that our thoughts can affect our attitudes and moods. It also suggests that we can change our thoughts by what we remember. We can think about things that bring out the feelings we want to feel.

So think, for a moment, about your favorite things as you reflect again on the words of Philippians 4:8:

Whatever is true,
whatever is honorable,
whatever is just,
whatever is pure,
whatever is pleasing,
whatever is gracious,
if there is any excellence,
if there is anything worthy of praise

... think about these things.

For now, let us consider excellence. Excellent things can often be your favorite things. If one of your favorite things is hiking in the woods, you will look for an excellent forest with excellent paths (or maybe no paths at all, if you like to go off the trail). If one of your favorite things is raindrops on roses, you will probably want to seek out or grow an excellent rose bush, maybe even a whole rose garden. If one of your favorite things is certain foods, you will probably be glad to discover a wonderful turkey dinner offered by a nearby church, or a really great restaurant. If one of your favorite things is music, you may want to find an excellent instrument to play or an opportunity to hear that music played by a talented musician. And if one of your favorite things is singing, you will want to find a choir or a group that sings your favorite songs.

At any time, we can celebrate the excellent things in our midst. What makes those things so excellent is the excellent effort provided to make them happen or the excellent Creator who has provided so lavishly in making our glorious surroundings. It is those things that are uncommon, uncommonly good, extraordinary, that we proclaim as excellent. A rare experience, a choice opportunity, a most wonderful service: These are excellent things. We would give them high grades, gold stars, blue ribbons.

Another way of describing excellence is as the best. In the book of Numbers, we are told, "You must present, as the Lord's portion, the best and holiest part of everything given to you" (18:29 NIV). In other words, give God your best, and do your best for Him. Don't be half-hearted when it comes to faith. What you do for God should be far better than mediocre; it should be something God would be glad, happy, pleased with. It should be something you, yourself, take pride in.

Although God will accept even our meagre little offerings, the way parents will accept the imperfect artwork of their child and post it on the refrigerator with magnets, God deserves quality, not inferiority. Too often, we all fall short of our calling and get caught in a pattern of what is adequate (to us) or tolerable or second-rate. Isaiah was called to pronounce judgment against this state of ordinariness and said, "Keep listening, but do not comprehend; keep looking, but do not perceive" (6:9). Live up to the challenge of being excellent for God (or for others' sake, for that matter). Isaiah was told to make the people know that their mind was dull, their ears were stopped, and their eyes were shut (Isaiah 6:10). The people were unable to see it, but it was proclaimed by the seraphim in Isaiah's vision that "the whole earth is full of God's glory" (Isaiah 6:3). It is a heavy heart that can't see the forest because the trees are in the way. "If I have told you about earthly things and you do not believe, how can you believe if I tell you about heavenly things?" (John 3:12). And God, through Isaiah, was asking, "Whom shall I send?" (6:8).

In the midst of our mediocrity, from the burden of our inadequacy, God calls us. He calls us all. And we say, "Woe is me" (Isaiah 6:5), because we feel so unqualified. But God takes us in our inability and makes us able. I don't know who said it first, but it seems relevant to call up the quote: "God does not call the qualified; God qualifies the called." This is a good message to everyone who feels that they couldn't possibly do anything extraordinary because they don't feel faithful enough. No one ever starts out faithful enough from a human point of view. Isaiah certainly felt unqualified, but then he said, "Here am I; send me" (6:8). God takes us in our gross imperfection and touches us in very special ways: "Now that this has touched your lips, your guilt has departed, and your sin is blotted out" (6:7), and then God calls us to do our best. "For you have died, and your life is hidden with Christ in God" (Colossians 3:3). "If you have been raised with Christ, seek the things that are above, where Christ is, seated at the right hand of God. Set your minds on things that are above, not on things that are on earth" (Colossians 3:1- 2).

And with your mind set upon the excellence of God, your eyes will behold that the whole earth is full of God's glory.

We should never feel as though we don't qualify: "If you have faith the size of a mustard seed, you will say to this mountain, 'Move from here to there,' and it will move; and nothing will be impossible for you" (Matthew 17:20). A little bit of faith can go a long way. Keep walking the walk, and you will soon walk very well.

What is excellent can be described as things that are glorious. "On the glorious splendor of Your majesty, and on Your wondrous works, I will meditate.... All Your works shall give thanks to You,O Lord, and all Your faithful shall bless You! They shall speak of the glory of Your Kingdom, and tell of Your power, to make known to all people Your mighty deeds, and the glorious splendor of Your Kingdom" (Psalm 145:5, 10- 12). And the kingdom of heaven is described in glorious terms, with excellent jewels and excellent light, excellent peace, and excellent love.

Love. In chapter 12 of Paul's first letter to the faithful of Corinth, he proclaims the variety of gifts in the Body of Christ and then urges them to "strive for the greater gifts" (31a), and even then, he goes on to say that there is still a "still more excellent way" (31b). Then, in chapter 13, he tells them the way of love: "Love is patient; love is kind; love is not envious or boastful, or arrogant or rude; it does not insist on its own way; it is not irritable or resentful; it does not rejoice in wrongdoing, but rejoices in the truth. It bears all things, believes all things, hopes all things, and endures all things. Love never ends" (1 Corinthians 13:4-8). Love is excellent.

And to the Christians in Philippi, Paul wrote, "This is my prayer, that your love may overflow more and more with knowledge and full insight, to help you to determine what is best, so that in the Day of Christ you may be pure and blameless, having produced the harvest of righteousness that comes through Jesus Christ for the glory and praise of God" (Philippians 1:9-11).

Later in Philippians, and I've discussed this before, Paul said, "Not that I have already obtained all this, or have already reached the goal, but I press on to make it my own, because Christ Jesus has made me His own. Beloved, I do not consider that I have made it my own; but this one thing I do: Forgetting what lies behind and straining forward to what lies ahead, I press on toward the goal for the prize of the heavenly call of God in Christ Jesus" (3:12-14). In Methodism, there is a heritage of striving for perfection. Please note: It is not about perfectionism. That can be more about obsessive behavior and distorted expectations than a life of faith. The goal for which we are to strive it to be "perfected in love."

And Jesus said, "No one has a greater love than this: to lay down one's life for one's friends" (John 15: 13).

John Wesley, Methodism's founder, wrote a treatise called *A Plain Account of Christian Perfection*. The goal for all God's children is sanctification, becoming mature Christians, seeking holiness of heart and life, becoming perfect in love. After justification, becoming right with God through grace, conversion, new birth, salvation. God isn't finished with us yet. Christ provides sanctifying grace. The grace to make us holy. It is seen in our spiritual growth and the maturity of our faith walk. And it is particularly known in what Wesley called "striving for perfection."

Perfection. Excellence. The best. The greatest. The glorious. The loving. There are things that are so excellent that they are considered treasures. But Jesus said, "Do not store up for yourselves treasures on earth, where moth and rust consume and where thieves break in and steal; but store up for yourselves treasures in heaven, …for where your treasure is, there will your heart be also" (Matthew 6:19-21). "Set your minds on things that are above" (Colossians 3:2).

But how do we lay up treasure in heaven? Could it begin with rising above the inability to hear and understand, to see and not perceive, as exposed by Isaiah? Could it begin when we truly recognize that the earth is full of God's glory? Couldn't it begin with belief? With trust? In spite of the weakness of our extraordinarily imperfect human minds, God has given us grace to believe. God said, "My grace is sufficient for you, for power is made perfect in weakness" (2

Corinthians 12:9). By believing, we embark on a new way of understanding, a new way of perceiving. As Peter said in 1 Corinthians 1:8 (NIV), "Though you have not seen Him, you love Him; and even though you do not see Him now, you believe in Him and are filled with inexpressible and glorious joy." "Obtaining, as the outcome of your faith, the salvation of your souls" (1 Corinthians 1:9 NAS). But Paul adds, "Not that I have already obtained this, or am already perfect; but I press on to make it my own because Christ Jesus has made me His own" (Philippians 3:12 ESV). Striving for perfection.

The way to lay up treasure in heaven is to live for the kingdom of God, to make it real in your midst, to practice a life of faith in such a way that your example and efforts will bring people to Christ, make them citizens of that kingdom and members of Christ's Body on earth. It is saved souls that find a home in heaven. Our purpose as disciples is to make disciples of all nations. And we can do this because the authority of Christ gives us the ability to do so: "All authority in heaven and on earth has been given to me. Go therefore, and make disciples of all nations, baptizing them in the name of the Father and of the Son and of the Holy Spirit, and teaching them to obey everything I have commanded you. And remember, I am with you always, to the end of the age" (Matthew 28:18- 20).

But it all begins with believing in Jesus Christ.

To inspire you to think about excellence, study what is in the scriptures:

"Who has known the mind of the Lord, so as to instruct him? But we have the mind of Christ" (1 Corinthians 2:16).

"If you have been raised with Christ, seek the things that are above, where Christ is, seated at the right hand of God. Set your minds on things that are above, not on things that are on earth.. For you have died, and your life is hidden with Christ in God. When Christ who is your life is revealed, then you also will be revealed with him in glory" (Colossians 3:1-4).

"Whatever your task, put yourselves into it, as done for the Lord, and not for your masters" (Colossians 3:23).

"You are a chosen race, a royal priesthood, a holy nation, God's own people; in order that you may proclaim the mighty acts of him who has called you out of darkness into his marvelous light" (1 Peter 2:9).

"Daniel distinguished himself above all the other presidents and satraps, because an excellent spirit was in him"(Daniel 6:3).

"Show yourself in all respects a model of good works, and in your teaching show integrity, gravity, and sound speech that cannot be censured; then any opponent will be put to shame, having nothing evil to say of us" (Titus 2:7).

"God's divine power has given us everything needed for life and godliness, through the knowledge of him who called us by his own glory and goodness Thus He has given us, through these things, his precious and very great promises, so that through them you may escape from the corruption that is in the world because of lust, and may become partakers of the divine nature" (2 Peter 1:3-4).

"Strive for the greater gifts. And I will show you a still more excellent way" (1 Corinthians 12:31).

"They were astonished beyond measure, saying, 'He has done everything well. He even makes the deaf to hear and the mute to speak'" (Mark 7:37).

"The law of the LORD is perfect, reviving the soul; the decrees of the LORD are sure, making wise the simple" (Psalm 19:7).

"Well done, good and trustworthy slave. You have been trustworthy in a few things; I will put you in charge of many things. Enter into the joy of your master" (Matthew 25:23).

"Therefore, my beloved, be steadfast, immovable, always excelling in the work of the Lord, because you know that in the Lord your labor is not in vain"(1 Corinthians 15:58).

"Let us not grow weary in doing what is right, for we will reap at harvest time, if we do not give up" (Galatian 6:9).

"Blessed is anyone who endures temptation. Such a one has stood the test and will receive the crown of life that the Lord has promised to those who love him"(James 1:12).

"I press on toward the goal for the prize of the heavenly call of God in Christ Jesus" (Philippians 3:14).

"Have this mind among yourselves, which is yours in Christ Jesus, who, though he was in the form of God, did not count equality with God a thing to be grasped, but emptied himself, by taking the form of a servant, being born in the likeness of men. And being found in human form he humbled himself and became obedient unto death, even death on a cross. Therefore God has highly exalted him and bestowed on him the name which is above every name, so that at the name of Jesus every knee should bow, in heaven and on earth and under the earth, and every tongue confess that Jesus Christ is Lord, to the glory of God the Father" (Philippians 2:5-11 ESV).

"Humble yourselves before the Lord, and he will exalt you" (James 4:10).

"Many who are first will be last, and the last will be first" (Matthew 19:30).

Stories

There is a television show called Dancing with the Stars where celebrities of various backgrounds of fame partner with professional ballroom dancers to compete for prizes. The stars might be athletes, actors, singers, musicians, or even famous businesspeople. Some have a fair degree of dancing talent before they begin; others need a lot of work. It is also a bit of a popularity contest, as viewers are able to phone in votes for their favorite dancers, who may not actually be the best performers. Expert judges sit and score each dance, giving critiques of the couples' performance. As the season progresses, some stars make amazing strides in improvement, actually becoming excellent dancers. But it takes hard work and serious efforts to score perfect 10s from the judges.

First place awards are given for many reasons. In track and field, where athletes race or compete in various field events, there is the Olympics. In football, it's the Super Bowl. In baseball, the World Series. And so on. Champions work hard, practicing almost every day in order to improve and become their best. In the same manner, we all need to practice our faith and become the best Christians we can be.

Long ago, during my college years, I worked in a restaurant as a cook's helper. That meant, mostly, helping to serve the food on the plates for the waitresses and waiters. My friend, Fred, worked there too. He wanted to be in the restaurant business, and he was always observing and imagining how things could improve. As important as the dining area is at a restaurant, the kitchen is the real soul of such a business. He would talk about all the things he might do differently to make things better, hoping one day that he would oversee a restaurant that wasfar superior, where not only the diners were happy with the wonderful food, but the servers and kitchen workers and chefs, and even those in the dish room, were glad to be there.

John Greenlees was the old man who ran the bowling alley at the Winnetka Community House. He taught me how to bowl, and I got pretty good. I loved it because of that. But he taught me something else.

One night, when I was struggling to keep my curve under control, he told me what I had to do to correct things I was doing wrong.

"It's not working," I complained. And I started to blame him for his wrong advice.

He told me, "I can't roll the ball for you. You've got to do it yourself. I can tell you how to do it right, but you need to concentrate to make it perfect."

My next ball was a strike. I finally got it. I never bowled a perfect game, but I bowled a lot of 200s. In fact, the first time Carol saw me bowl, I got a 220.

Carol and I fell in love in the spring as the trees were turning green; certain paths we walked are strongly imprinted in my mind, making them some of my favorite things.

When our son, Tim, was a senior, we moved to a new town, where I would serve a different United Methodist church as their pastor. The school had a talent contest, and Tim played his electric guitar. He performed two songs that morning and did very nicely. For his third number, he began instrumentally with several riffs until they led into a chord progression, and he stepped up to the microphone and sang an amazing rendition of "The House of the Rising Sun," voice and guitar taking us away. He had practiced more than I knew. And he won fifty dollars in that talent contest. It created a wonderful in for him in his new school. I felt like I was awesome because, of course, in that moment, I was living vicariously through Tim. Excellent.

Emily, our daughter, was an excellent speller. I don't think she practiced spelling; words just always came very naturally. My children are both very smart (I married the right genes). She could read almost anything when she was five years old.

When she won her middle school spelling bee, we were quite proud. That qualified her for a regional spelling bee. Again, living vicariously through my children, I oozed pride every time she spelled the word given to her. I was almost unable to sit still when she was still on stage with only two other students; she finally misspelled a word and came in third, which is still excellent.

What to Do

Make a list of some of your favorite things. Actually write them down. Add to them over time. Revise it as you are inspired. Refer to it when you're feeling down. Let the remembrance of them work in your heart. What about each of these things makes it one of your favorites? I have always loved a simple walk in the woods, especially during the autumn colors.

Practice. Get good at what you can do. Whether it is an athletic event, a musical instrument, or public speaking. It could be knitting or sewing or craft-making. It could be cooking or decorating cakes. The more you do something, the better you get.

Practice your faith. Don't just feel it; talk about it. Do it . Tell others how excellent Jesus is. This doesn't happen as much as it should. People are afraid of being rejected for being self-righteous or for their listeners just rejecting the truth. They don't want to offend others who might feel like you're being condescending. Don't talk about their sinfulness and the need for repentance; talk about whatever is excellent about faith.

Do those things that Jesus called us to do. Be mission-minded.

One woman and I initiated a fellowship committee in our church. One of the things she organized was a monthly community senior potluck. She arranged for special speakers, musicians, or politicians to be present and give a program. This has become an ongoing excellent event in that congregation.

Love, according to 1 Corinthians 12:31, is "the more excellent way." Memorize 1 Corinthians 13. Repeat it to yourself often. Notice that faith, without love, is nothing (1 Corinthians 13:2). Be patient with others; be kind; do not be jealous or boastful or arrogant or rude; do not insist on your own way; do not be resentful; and do not rejoice in what is wrong.

Be persistent. In high school, I was the shot-putter on the track team. In order to heave the twelve-pound shot, there were some very difficult motions I had to make. But the more I practiced them, the more they eventually became natural, and I got pretty good. I may not have been excellent enough to win a lot of blue ribbons, but I earned many second and third place points for the team.

A Song

Dear Lord, help us be what You want us to be.
Open our hearts that our eyes may see.
Open our minds that our hearts may know.
And open our souls that our love may show.

Move us with peace and shape our desire
and give us the hope that a faith can inspire.
And give us a faith that will burn with a light
that will shine upon others and give them more sight.

Move us beyond just some hope for a sign
and help us believe there's a spark that's
 divine so deeply within us, so silently still,
awaiting the touch of the truth of Your will.

Let it burst into flames til it sets itself free
and makes us the image we're created to be.

A Prayer

    Dear Lord, You are not done with any of us yet. Continue to shape us. Transform us by the renewing of our minds so that we may prove what is excellent. Give us discerning minds so that we may know what is best in Creation and in action. And help us do what it takes to make this world better for the sake of Your glory, and for the sake of generations yet to come. This we pray in Jesus's name. Amen.

CHAPTER EIGHT

If there is anything worthy of Praise

Let everything that breathes praise the LORD.
PSALM 150:6

At the beginning of this book on the heavenly mind, I suggested that we would not just be entertaining ideas with our minds, but we would be contemplating the things that could positively affect the soul. The setting of faith provides much more than just positive thinking (although it can be that). It is where heavenly thoughts can be evoked, for "as a person thinketh in their heart, so are they" (Proverbs 23:7 KJV). What, then, are the thoughts of your heart? Realize that your thoughts affect your inner nature, your spiritual being. Realize that what you think influences, to a great degree, what you become, what you do, what you are. Realize, especially, that your mind is related to your soul, and your state of mind can affect the state of your soul.

Knowing this, we have considered issues revolving around those things Paul tells us to think about. In Philippians 4:8, he says:

Whatever is true,
whatever is honorable,
whatever is just,
whatever is pure,
whatever is pleasing,

> whatever is gracious,
> if there is any excellence,
> if there is anything worthy of praise...
> think about these things.

We have considered all but the last of these subjects. Now, let us apply our minds to those things that are worthy of praise, and consider foremost the kingdom of God.

Who is greatest in the kingdom of God? Who is the most worthy of praise? When Jesus hears this question while talking to his disciples, He responds in a rather cryptic way. His style, to say the least, is rather baffling, because He turns all the common, worldly expectations either upside down or sideways. He placed a child in their midst and said, "Truly, I tell you, unless you change and become like children, you will never enter the Kingdom of Heaven" (Matthew 18:3). "And a little child shall lead them" (Isaiah 11:6). A little child shall be their example, their model, their standard for living a faithful life. A little child in the midst of adults, intimidated, feeling insignificant, feeling small. A little child shall lead them?

It's difficult to discern exactly what Jesus may have meant at that moment. We don't know if it was a one-year-old or a five-year-old. Perhaps He was indicating the humility of the child, embarrassed in front of all those adults. Or would the child have felt proud to become the center of attention? (Could that have been a fun moment for the child? Did the child know Jesus?) Perhaps Jesus wanted to make an appeal to innocence or to the childlike qualities of the uninhibited enjoyment of life, or to the simplicity of childish desires, or even to the unmixed priorities of early life. All seem relevant for the disciple of Christ. But the message becomes mixed when those positive qualities, considered virtues, are placed alongside some of the qualities of childishness, which are not so virtuous. One thing that is true, however, about children is that they need praise and encouragement.

Children do not need flattery (though to a small child, flattery might be the same as praise). But children need encouragement. The intention is not to feed ego-centered ambition but to foster enthusiasm. We should not just affirm positive qualities, but we should validate positive experiences. Praising children not only builds their self-esteem, it shows approval. It is not done to bring acclaim but to build confidence. The applause is not something offered only when it is merited, but for the sake of acceptance.

"Like newborn infants, long for the pure, spiritual milk, so that by it you may grow into salvation; if indeed you have tasted that the Lord is good" (1 Peter 2:2-3). Long for acceptance, long for the good feeling of knowing the essential Gospel, the pure spiritual milk of knowing that Jesus is the Christ, and that He died for your sins, and that your sins are forgiven. You are accepted, from the point of view of heaven. "And a little child shall lead them" (Isaiah 11:6 NKJV). "For you have tasted that the Lord is good." You taste it in the acceptance you feel; in the approval of others; in the encouraging words of others; in the praise you have received. "By it you may grow into salvation."

One of the most common ways of showing praise is to offer a compliment. Children raised with little or no complimentary praise will feel like failures. And they will eventually seek it from another source, sometimes more contrary to our desires.

If you would "train children in the right way," so that "when old, they will not stray" (Proverbs 22:6), then children need encouragement, need to be affirmed, especially when they are taking steps in a new direction.

In one of the churches I served, the junior high youth loved to play a game called *Applause*. The game is played by sending one person out of the room, beyond earshot, while the rest of the group determines a certain task, an action, or a gesture, pose, or motion to be performed. When the person returns, he or she begins to move about doing certain things that might lead to completing the task still unknown to them, for example, scratching their head, or hopping on one foot. Of course, applause is offered when they enter. Then, as they move, the group claps for motions in the right direction. When there is no clapping, they know that's not what we want them to do. So they try something else, until some movement in the right direction begins, and the clapping keeps them going until they accomplish the task. Simple tasks, like picking up a book, standing on one foot, or sitting cross-legged on the floor (one boy even tried slapping himself, imagining that to be the task we wanted him to do).

But the applause influences the direction someone moves. Part of the problem in modern culture is that we are applauding too many wrong things. If there is anything worthy of praise, it is faith, morality, decency, depth of character, kindness, and goodness. Excellence is worthy of praise. It is praiseworthy to be involved in the kingdom of God. It praiseworthy to know that Jesus Christ is King and that we are His subjects. It is knowing the cross, its forgiveness, grace, God's redemption, Christ's exaltation, the Resurrection.

Too often, our culture behaves as if all the wrong things are commendable, like drinking and drug use, promiscuity, defying authority, and self-righteousness. There may be no audible clapping for all of these things, but many wrong directions are being taken, maybe, because there's just been no clapping at all. The right directions are unknown, and there is too little encouragement.

Praise. Compliments. If you can't say anything nice, don't say anything at all (Thumper's father). One man, who claims to try to live up to this maxim, once told me, "I really like all the dumb things you say in your sermons."

Once I heard two women talking about a preacher's wife, who was so wonderful and sweet and beautiful and kind. One said to the other, "You know, I bet there's no one you could mention to her and she couldn't find something good to say about them."

The other said, "I bet I could think of someone she won't say anything good about."

"You're on," said the first.

They caught up to her after one worship service, and the second woman said, "What do you think about Satan?"

"Well," said the preacher's wife, "he is always working. Never rests."

A little boy wanted to do his best to live up to the same ideal: If you can't say anything nice, don't say anything at all. But he just didn't like his second grade teacher. Finally, he figured out what to say: "Miss Jones, you're the best second grade teacher I've ever had."

Praise. Jesus put the child in their midst and told His disciples, who were eager to know who might be the greatest in heaven, that they would never even know unless they become like children. Children need praise. But they quickly feel out of place among adults. They don't feel like they are as important as those big people. And I believe that's the crux of Jesus's lesson because the very next thing He says, "Whoever becomes humble like this child is the greatest in the Kingdom of Heaven" (Matthew 18:4).

Elsewhere, Jesus says, "Many who are first will be last, and the last first" (Matthew 19:30), and "The last will be first, and the first will be last" (20:16). The journey of life is not about feeling important, about being number one (I wish high school athletic coaches would learn that). If it's importance you want in life, as far as heaven is concerned, you're unimportant, you're last. Heaven is about helping others feel good about themselves, though. It's about treating others as better than yourself, the way a child tends to think about adults.

A special word about humility needs to be said here. Sometimes, seeking greatness is a solitary endeavor; one person tries to be greater than another. It creates a competitive environment and causes a distance between people. Realize that when there is competition, somebody has to lose. And though losing can be a good test of sportsmanlike character, how would you feel if you lost all the time? Dorotheos of Gaza, a sixth-century monk, gives an illustration of how our purpose in this life could look. If our lives include greatness, that greatness is not meant to be for the individual, but for the whole. He envisions a wheel with multiple spokes. The wheel is life. God is at the center, the hub around which everything must move. The spokes of the wheel are the paths of human lives. To move closer to God is to move closer to others. And to move closer to others is to move closer to God. To move away from others is to move away from God. Likewise, to move away from God is to move away from others. But it is in Him we live and move and have our being (Acts 17:28).

Humble people do not seek their own advancement but the advancement of the whole. "If there is any encouragement in Christ, any consolation from love, any sharing in the Spirit, any compassion and sympathy, make my joy complete: be of the same mind, having the same love, being in full accord and of one mind. Do nothing from selfish ambition or conceit, but in humility regard others as better than yourselves. Let each of you look not to your own interests, but to the interests of the others" (Philippians 2:1-4).

If there is anything worthy of praise, it is the act of giving praise, sincere praise. Think about it. And think about how you could try to give a word of encouragement to others, no matter who they are. Everybody needs it. Think about this: If this was the last time you were going to see someone, what would you want to say to them? If you might never see them again, what would you want them to hear from you? And even though it is said that Christians never see each other for the last time, here's one way of looking at life in the world that makes every moment look great: Treat every moment as though it might be your last. Then, every moment can be a moment of triumph for Christ, a moment of victory for our King, as the King lives through you.

To inspire you to think about things that are worthy of praise, study what is in the scriptures:

"'Worthy is the Lamb that was slaughtered, to receive power and wealth and wisdom and might and honor and glory and blessing!' Then I heard every creature in heaven, and on earth, and under the earth, and under the sea, and all that is in them, singing: 'To the one seated on the throne, and to the Lamb, be blessing and honor and glory and might forever and ever'" (Revelation 5:12-13).

"May I never boast of anything except the cross of our Lord Jesus Christ, by which the world has been crucified to me, and I to the world" (Galatians 6:14).

"Through Him then, let us continually offer a sacrifice of praise to God, that is, the fruit of lips that confess His name" (Hebrews 13:15).

"Great is the LORD, and greatly to be praised, His greatness is unsearchable" (Psalm 145:3).

"I call upon the LORD, who is worthy to be praised, and I am saved from my enemies" (2 Samuel 22:4).

"The people whom I formed for Myself... declare My praise" (Isaiah 43:21).

"My tongue shall tell of our righteousness and of Your praise all day long" (Psalm 35:28).

"Praise the LORD. Praise God in his sanctuary; praise Him in his mighty firmament. Praise him for his mighty deeds; praise him according to his surpassing greatness! Praise him with trumpet sound, praise him with lute and harp! Praise him with tambourine and dance; praise him with strings and pipe! Praise him with clanging cymbals, praise him with loud clashing cymbals. Let everything that breathes praise the LORD. Praise the LORD" (Psalm 150:1-6).

There are quite a few psalms that echo the idea of praising God, including Psalms 18, 21, 28, 30, 32, 34, 36, 40, 41, 66, 105, 106, 111, 113, 116, 117, 135, 136, 138, 146, and 147.

"God has destined us not for wrath but for obtaining salvation through our Lord Jesus Christ, who died for us, so that whether we are awake or asleep, we may live with him. Therefore encourage one another and build up each other, as indeed you are doing" (1 Thessalonians 5:9-11).

"But we appeal to you, brothers and sisters, to respect those who labor among you, and have charge of you in the Lord and admonish you; esteem them very highly in love because of their work" (1 Thessalonians 5:12-13).

Stories

"Start praising God and you cease to feel needy." It may not always be true, but I've suffered with kidney stones five different times. Praising God in those hours of suffering did not remove the agony, but it did help me keep perspective. When we can rejoice in every next breath God gives us; when we can be grateful for the paramedics' arrival and for the hope to live beyond this moment of anguish; when we can still celebrate the fact that our eyes still see and our ears still hear, we not only gain a new outlook, but I believe it honors God.

Paul also suffered a recurring "thorn in the flesh": "I must go on boasting. Although there is nothing to be gained, I will go on to visions and revelations from the Lord. I know a man in Christ who fourteen years ago was caught up to the third heaven. Whether it was in the body or out of the body I do not know- God knows. And I know that this man-whether in the body or apart from the body I do not know, but God knows-was caught up to paradise and heard inexpressible things, things that no one is permitted to tell. I will boast about a man like that, but I will not boast about myself, except about my weaknesses. Even if I should choose to boast, I would not be a fool, because I would be speaking the truth. But I refrain, so no one will think more of me than is warranted by what I do or say, or because of these surpassingly great revelations. Therefore, in order to keep me from becoming conceited, I was given a thorn in my flesh, a messenger of Satan, to torment me. Three times I pleaded with the Lord to take it away from me. But He said to me, 'My grace is sufficient for you, for my power is made perfect in weakness.' Therefore I will boast all the more gladly about my weaknesses, so that Christ's power may rest on me. That is why, for Christ's sake, I delight in weaknesses, in insults, in hardships, in persecutions, in difficulties. For when I am weak, then I am strong" (2 Corinthians 9:1-10 NIV). Boasting is like praising. When we boast in our own experiences, we are praising ourselves. But when we boast in God's graciousness to us, we are praising God.

Joseph's story is worthy to note. Like Daniel, there was an excellent spirit within him. Joseph was treated poorly by his own brothers, sold into slavery in Egypt, and even put in Pharaoh's prison. But he excelled, first as Potiphar's accountant and then as he offered service to other prisoners. As he interpreted dreams, he was so commended that he was eventually called on to interpret Pharaoh's dream. As a reward, he ended up second only to Pharaoh. When his brothers came to Egypt, he looked beyond their cruelty to him and saw God's purpose in all that happened (Genesis 37-50).

The inspirational stories in chapter 5 are about people doing things that are worthy of praise. But consider deeds of heroism by doctors and nurses in hospitals, paramedics and other first responders, like firefighters and police: They deserve praise. I even thank the sanitary hauler for taking away my garbage. Don't ever take that for granted.

Those in the military deserve our praise. Although war does not deserve praise, the idea of defending the oppressed and defending our own nation has merit.

Heroism: The man who tackled the gunman, the one who took the bullet to save another, the one who jumped on the tracks to rescue the child who fell off the platform, the group of strangers who pulled together to lift a car that had crashed and rolled onto a bystander, the protesters who affected change, the lifeguard who rescued the drowning girl. Many examples of heroic action deserve our praise.

But even common heroes, like the teachers who educate our children, the coaches who train us, the parents who care for their kids, and the grandparents who show so much love also deserve praise.

What to do

Praise God for the saving grace you've experienced, and especially for the Savior, for the forgiveness you've received, for the healing you've experienced, and for all the blessings you can recall.

Boast about your church, your worship experience, the preacher's message, the choir's singing, and so on. Let others know how wonderful it is to be there. Praise God for the faith experiences you can share.

Worship. Nothing brings God more praise and glory than when we present ourselves, heart, mind, soul, and body, before His presence. God created the church for this purpose.

Offer compliments whenever you can. A compliment can bless a person and make their day. Praise them for their example or for whatever they might have done that is worthy of commending.

Praise the children around you for everything good they accomplish. If they got good grades (even if their grades aren't so good, let them know you are proud that they are learning; grades aren't the only measure of knowledge), if they did a special project, if they played an instrument, whatever; don't hesitate to build their confidence. If you see them in worship, commend them. Remember, we are to "build up each other" (1 Thessalonians 5:11).

October is Pastor Appreciation Month. Give a love gift. Recognize them as a blessing, at a minimum, for having entered into the ministry of grace. Not every sermon will ring your bell, but surely, there have been some good words.

Give church leaders a word of appreciation now and then. A thank-you note can make their day and encourage them to carry on.

Volunteers should receive praise and thanks.

Teamwork can be praised. Whether it is the high school football team, long-distance runners, the tennis team, or the volleyball team, cheer them on. Never boo, even the opposing team.

Applaud any job well done.

A Song
A day will come when all the world
will take away their masks.
Party flags will be unfurled,
nd wine will leave its casks.
Everyone will join and dance
and sing the type of song
that captures others in a trance
and makes them sing along.
Some will say they dreamed the day.
Some will say they're free.
But I believe I'll simply say it's this that ought to be.
And I will say, it's no surprise
when you appear before my eyes.

A Prayer

O Lord, we may not appear as heroes to the world, but we are here. We may not be working miracles, but we are faithful, and we may never seek anything more than Your telling us, "Well done," but we are doing Your will. Help us to give honor where honor is due, praise where praise is due, and glory, always, to You. Give us gracious hearts that we may be generous with our gratitude; positive minds that we may see worthiness when it has happened; and hopeful spirits that we may gladly look upon this world and rejoice. In Jesus's name we pray. Amen.

CHAPTER NINE

Set your Mind on the Things of the Spirit

> Those who live according to the Spirit set their minds set on the things of the Spirit
> -ROMANS 8:5B

How has the Holy Spirit been working in your life? What has the Holy Spirit been doing around you?

Many don't really know how to answer questions like these because they simply don't know how to recognize how the Holy Spirit works in this world; they don't really know what the Spirit does or can do. If we can begin to name the things of the Spirit, I think we can answer some of these questions. And we can eventually begin to understand the Baptism of the Holy Spirit.

"Anyone who does not have the Spirit of Christ, does not belong to Him" (Romans 8:9b).

Truth. John 16:13 says, "When the Spirit of Truth comes, He will guide you into all the truth."

We experience the Holy Spirit when we experience truth.
Imagine a brick wall blocking out the light. Truth comes to remove the bricks, one by one, until light can flood through. Sight. "I pray that the God of our Lord Jesus Christ, the Father

of glory, may give you a spirit of wisdom and revelation as you come to know Him, so that with the eyes of your heart enlightened, you may know what is the hope to which he has called you, what are the riches of his glorious inheritance among the saints, and the immeasurable greatness of His power for us who believe" (Ephesians 1:17- 19). The KJV says, "The eyes of your understanding being opened." The Living Bible says, "Your hearts will be flooded with light."

We experience the Holy Spirit, the spirit of truth, when we experience anything that creates a spark of understanding in our minds, a spark of knowing, a spark of wisdom.

Life. In John 10:10, we hear, "I came that they might have life, and have it abundantly."

We experience the Holy Spirit when we experience our aliveness.

Imagine a seed. A seed is like a spark of life. What sort of seeds are you planting? Seeds are beginnings. Seeds can symbolize new life.

Sometimes, the way we begin will determine where we end. Our interests and focus will determine the kind of person we will be. If we set too much emphasis on the things of the flesh, we will probably not have much of a spiritual life. But to set the mind on the Spirit is life and peace (Romans 8:6b).

We will reap what we sow: "The one who sows sparingly will also reap sparingly, and the one who sows bountifully will also reap bountifully" (2 Corinthians 9:6). "Do not be deceived; God is not mocked. For you reap whatever you sow. If you sow to your own flesh, you will reap corruption from the flesh; but if you sow to the Spirit, you will reap eternal life from the Spirit" (Galatians 6:7- 8).

Seeds must be nurtured. The things of the spirit can be nurtured by the ways we set our minds on them. Thinking about them, meditating on them, is like watering the seeds. By focusing our thoughts on life and truth, more and more bricks will be removed. And that light also helps the seeds we sow to grow after they germinate. "Speaking the truth in love, we must grow up in every way into Him who is the Head, into Christ" (Ephesians 4:15). Seeds are supposed to grow. Then, by growing, the plant becomes more and more mature, until it produces fruit, more seeds. And, often, not just once.

We experience the Holy Spirit as we grow, as we experience moments that enlighten and enliven us, as we experience times in our lives that quicken us, and we feel alive, more alive. We experience growth as we behold those compelling wonders that evoke awe and inspiration. Sparks.

Grace. John 1:14, 16, 17 says, "And the Word became flesh and lived among us, and we have seen his glory, the glory as of a father's only Son, full of grace and truth ... from His fullness we have all received, grace upon grace.... Grace and truth came through Jesus Christ."

We experience the Holy Spirit when we experience grace.

We experience the Holy Spirit not only through the influence of truth but also through the wonders of God's grace. Grace could be another name for the things of the Spirit. Imagine a garden. Our life is a garden. Flowers and fruits are gifts of God through His great Creation that can perpetuate life. "Each of us was given grace according to the measure of Christ's gift" (Ephesians 4:7). First of all, the measure of

Christ's gift is immeasurable. Remember: "I came that they may have life, and have it abundantly" (John 10:10). Second, there is a purpose for those gifts: "to equip the saints for the work of ministry, for the building up of the Body of Christ, until all of us come to the unity of the faith and the knowledge of the Son of God, to maturity, to the measure of the full stature of Christ" (Ephesians 4:12-13). When we grow and mature, we will build, build up, and augment the Body of Christ, the church, and the fellowship of believers. We are to build one another up (1 Thessalonians 5:11).

The Spirit moves by the grace of God. We cannot cause the Spirit to move, but we can accept its movement, and we can prepare ourselves to receive it. That's why we "think about these things."

That's why we set our minds on the things of the Spirit. But God's Spirit is inseparable from God's grace. They are not one and the same, but one reveals the other, as in "where there's smoke, there's fire." The experience of the Spirit of God, and the things of the Spirit, can be known through anything that enables us to move toward God, to respond to the moving of the Spirit in our lives. Please note: Our purpose is not just to be moved or to be inspired. We are to respond. I've known several people who have claimed to be spiritual simply because they were inspired. Inspired for what? To feel inspired? No. We are inspired by the things of the Spirit in order to act. And if the inspiration you feel does not move you in love to embrace others, you may be resisting it. So go to church and worship. And go into the world and serve.

The Holy Spirit is working in us before we know it or recognize it. This is what John Wesley called prevenient grace. It can be known through the experience of a conscience, which is a sort of built-in morality detector, and part of our likeness to God. Prevenient grace can also work through creation to inspire us. But we can resist it. We can deny our conscience; we can take that beautiful sunrise for granted, or we can disclaim the awe that otherwise might make us say, "Wow!" We can turn our backs on the light, separate ourselves from the glorious gifts that are right before us, and never nurture those seeds. We can resist God's grace by setting our minds on the things of the flesh, on earthly delights that do not nurture the spirit of faith within us. We can resist spiritual rebirth.

But when we do not resist, when we yield to the moving of God's grace, we are changed. The light shines through. We grow in love and grace, in graciousness. We are set free from sin and begin to live in holiness, righteousness, and peace. It is glorious.

John Wesley said that the work of the spirit is an inward impression upon the soul. Its ultimate purpose is where the Spirit of God directly witnesses to our spirit, witnessing that we are children of God, that Jesus Christ loves us and has given Himself for us, and that all our sins are blotted out, and we can say that "I, even I, am reconciled to God." Then, therefore, we will be loving; we will be reconciling; we will bear witness to this grace working in our lives and in the world. We will bear witness to God's saving grace.

We are setting our minds on the things of the Spirit.

A saved life begins with the first dawning of light upon the soul. That first ray of light can lead to others. Soon, inklings of God's will begin to evolve in our minds. Then, by grace, there is a wish to please God, and still then, there is a discovery of our distance from God, our state of fallenness, and the need for repentance.

But spiritual sight begins with the first revelations of these truths. They may seem like small truths, but if we begin to set our minds on these truths, we will grow in grace. It is spiritual sight to recognize the rainbow in every drop of water; to recognize the abundance of life in every blade of grass; and even then, to see God's magnificent graciousness in the fields, the harvest of crops, or a beautiful garden.

It is spiritual sight to be able to look at the awesomeness of the Grand Canyon or the majesty of the mountains and see the glorious touch of God's will in Creation, to gaze upon the stars above and acknowledge God's ever-present power reaching so far beyond us, and just wonder: How can such an amazing God be with us, with me, here? It is spiritual sight to look at a home and see togetherness; to look at a town and see community; to look at a city and see the overflowing resource of the likeness of God in all the people. It is spiritual sight to look at another and see another soul for whom Christ has died.

By spiritual sight, we can see the cross in every crossroad, the Crucifixion in every sacrificial act, and our wounded Savior in the suffering of another. That sight enables us to look at others and realize that there dwells the image of God, a likeness of the divine.

Are you growing in grace? Does the Spirit of God move in you in some of these ways? Does your spiritual sight-the enlightenment of your heart-enable you to feel more and more abundantly gifted, more and more able to recognize and do the things of the Spirit, the things of faith, the things of Christ? Can you rise to the challenge of using the gifts God is offering you as a mature believer? Are you on the way to being able to measure up to the status of the fullness of Christ?

Let your eyes, your spiritual eyes, be fully opened to see the wonderful things of the Spirit. And know that "if we live by the Spirit we will also walk by the Spirit" (Galatians 5:25 Darby).

To inspire you to think about setting your minds on the things of the Spirit, study what is in the scriptures:

"The fruit of the Spirit is love, joy, peace, patience, kindness, generosity, faithfulness, gentleness and self-control" (Galatians 5:22- 23).

"Through the Spirit, by faith, we eagerly wait for the hope of righteousness. For in Christ Jesus neither circumcision nor uncircumcision counts for anything; the only thing that counts is faith working through love" (Galatians 5:5-6).

"Live by the Spirit, I say, and do not gratify the desires of the flesh. For the flesh desires what is opposed to what the Spirit desires, and what the Spirit desires is opposed to the flesh; for these are opposed to each other, to prevent you from doing what you want" (Galatians 5:16-17).

"The works of the flesh are obvious: fornication, impurity, licentiousness, idolatry, sorcery, enmities, strife, jealousy, anger, quarrels, dissensions, factions, envy, drunkenness, carousing, and things like these. I am warning you, as I warned you before, that those who do such things will not inherit the kingdom of God" (Galatians 5:19-21).

"Therefore be imitators of God, as beloved children, and live in love, as Christ loved us and gave himself up for us, a fragrant offering and sacrifice to God" (Ephesians 5:1-2).

"Once you were darkness, but now in the Lord you are light. Live as children of light (for the fruit of the light is found in all that is good and right and true). Try to find out what is pleasing to the Lord. Take no part in the unfruitful works of darkness, but instead expose them" (Ephesians 5:8-11).

"The hour is coming, and is now here, when the true worshipers will worship the Father in spirit and truth, for the Father seeks such as these. God is spirit, and those who worship Him must worship in Spirit and truth" (John 4:23-24).

"Very truly, I tell you, no one can enter the kingdom of God without being born of water and the Spirit. What is born of the flesh is flesh, and what is born of the Spirit is spirit" (John 3:5-6).

Stories

Seeing an opportunity in his church to help the hungry through donations of food, a man took a closer look at the ministry. He saw what it did, how it helped people in need. He became inspired to be more involved. In another year, he was encouraging his congregation to participate more abundantly. The help he felt happening through his participation was a spiritual thing. Help: a thing of the spirit.

A woman who had retired felt that since she had more time, she could do more praying. The spirit moved her to establish a prayer ministry in her congregation. The ministry evolved. A branch of participants began a visitation ministry. Some ladies who loved to knit and crochet began making lap blankets for the elderly or shut-ins in their community. The comfort that all these ministries offered was a spiritual thing. Prayer and comfort: things of the spirit.

A man felt moved to get other men in his congregation to build desks for students in Africa, through the United Methodist Committee on Relief. The design and instructions were provided, and the men made ten desks. The mission was a thing of the spirit. And the collegiality and fellowship among the men was, likewise, a thing of the spirit. Fellowship and missions: things of the spirit.

A pastor felt inspired to preach about how God's power is made perfect in weakness (2 Corinthians 12:9). A woman on the fringe of the membership happened to attend worship that Sunday, and she felt strengthened and encouraged. She soon became a full member and was involved in many ways, doing whatever she could to strengthen the church. Her renewed strength was a thing of the spirit.

During an adult Sunday school class, a young man felt a strong conviction that urged him to go deeper. As he did, he felt filled with the Spirit and began to testify to the blessings God was working in his life, convincing many others of the relevance of faith and church life. Several people began attending worship with him, and many became strong members. That conviction was a thing of the Spirit.

What to do

Worship. In the body of believers filled with the Spirit, we can experience more of the things of the Spirit than in any other place. This is not to say that we will never experience grace at work in us elsewhere, but that the church, the gathering, is designed to be a spiritual encounter.

Find your niche. What are you passionate about? Is it hunger? Join a local hunger ministry. Get involved in a hunger walk. Work to raise awareness and funds for places where people are starving. Is it poverty? Likewise, do what you can to fight poverty. There are ministries and organizations locally, statewide, nationwide, and worldwide. If it is sexual assault, there are many ministries you can find; ask the police where one is needed most. What makes you angry? Get passionate. Immigration, race, and class relations are very hot issues today. Get involved.

Seek the spiritual reality in or through every experience. Whatever makes you feel that aha moment might be the Spirit's work. I've felt it in the sight of a sunrise, sunset, or gentle breeze; the beauty of creation, the shoreline, or the creek bank; as well as in the smile of another, an act of kindness, an offer of goodness, and a touch of love.

Think about your salvation. Dwell on it. Bask in it. Let the knowledge of God's saving grace pour over you now and then. It will refresh you, inspire you, and comfort you. Never take your salvation for granted. And realize that you are not saved, as if it were a once-and-for-all-time experience. No, you are being saved. If you are still in this world, God is apparently not finished with you. God is not finished with any of us yet.

So grow. Spiritual growth can and should keep happening in your life. If you feel as though you've got nothing left to learn, faith wise, don't believe it. I've known plenty of people who felt that as long as they had their ticket, they didn't need to do anything else. Well, if you're so spiritual, then who is listening to your words, who is following you and growing? How about teaching, then?

Think of yourself and others as souls on-the-way. Think, not just about their physical existence, as important as that is, since God made us with bodies, but think about their spiritual existence. That is the part of them that you will know for an eternity.

Walk in love. Be as loving as Christ was when He went to the cross. Make sacrifices for the sake of their salvation.

Contemplate the fruits of the spirit, as listed in Galatians 5. Set your mind on these things. Live in such a way that they are truly part of your character, your perceived virtues. Do not take them for granted. The seeds of faith should produce abundant fruit. Jesus said, "You will know them by their fruits" (Matthew 7:20).

Beware of spiritual exercises or activities that are not based solidly in Christianity. A lot of New Age and non-Christian (or quasi-Christian) groups offer spiritual experiences. Some groups are downright anti-- Christian; some mask themselves as compatible with the faith but can be an avenue for the demonic to be introduced.

Any religion that advocates death, killing, or destruction is a sick religion. Religion should be life-enriching. Never blame a certain group for the problems of the world. Nazi Germany did that with the Jews. You might just as well claim that it is redheads who are causing all the problems.

Be on fire. John Wesley supposedly said, "Set yourself on fire, and people will come just to watch you burn." Not a literal fire, not literally burning, obviously, but with passion.

A Song

> There always seems to be a face
> among the flames that make the fire.
> It's an image that we can't embrace,
> an answer to a great desire.
>
> To touch, to beckon to be real,
> and then behold what we could learn;
> we comprehend what we can feel,
> but as we come too close, we burn.
>
> There's shadows if we look away
> from what we know will keep us warm.
> They move and let our eyes betray
> the flicker for a darkened form.
>
> But blazes die and embers cool,

and life becomes a search for fuel.

A Prayer

Help me, Lord, to set my mind on the things of the spirit; to focus, to dedicate my ability to think on what You would have me think. And if my mind should stray from these things, bring me back. Should interruptions occur, let me see opportunities to love in them, moments of grace in them, and times for applying my thoughts to whatever may come. Above all, Lord, give me grace to see, through all I encounter, Your presence, Your touch, and Your purpose. This I pray in Jesus's name. Amen.

Conclusion

> We have the mind of Christ.
> 1 CORINTHIANS 2:16

With our minds, we think. With our minds, we believe. With our minds, we seek the blessings in life. That is why it is important to do as Paul suggests:

> Whatever is true,
> whatever is honorable,
> whatever is just,
> whatever is pure,
> whatever is pleasing,
> whatever is gracious,
> if there is any excellence,
> if there is anything worthy of praise
> ... think about these things.

My hope, through the reflections of the past nine chapters, is that something relevant has been shared, that something here has given you cause to think in a new way and focus your attention on the heavenly mind we possess as we begin to grow in Christ. We have the mind of Christ. We have a wonderful ability to choose to think about spiritual things. We can dedicate ourselves to thinking these thoughts. We can vow to take time to contemplate, to seriously consider them until they are all we ever think. We can intentionally pray about things that are true, honorable, just, pure, pleasing, gracious, excellent, and praiseworthy. When we make a promise, in some ways, we are hoping to affect the future. It is like investing in an exclusive path of decision- making, forsaking all other paths for the sake of a dedicated path.

When we dedicate ourselves to new ways of thinking, for example, we are imagining the abandonment of the old ways or, at least, reprioritizing them.

In 2 Corinthians 5:16-17, Paul said, "From now on, therefore, we regard no one from a human point of view; even though we once knew Christ from a human point of view, we know Him no longer in this way. So if anyone is in Christ, there is a new creation; everything old has passed away; see, everything has become new." "We regard no one from a human point of view": Our point of view can be altered by the grace of faith. Our old ways of thinking are no longer relevant, from the point of view of the Spirit. When we think of others, no matter who they are, we can think of them as souls for whom Jesus died. They need us to think of them this way. A sinner is lost. They need finding, and they need to find Christ. But we're lost too, and we also need to find Christ, again and again and again.

Though it may be true that "my thoughts are not your thoughts, nor are your ways my ways.... For as the heavens are higher than the earth, so are my ways higher than your ways and my thoughts than your thoughts" (Isaiah 55:8-9), it is also true that with Paul, by grace, we can "let the same mind be in [us] that was in Christ Jesus" (Philippians 2:5). Although God's thoughts do transcend human thoughts, I believe our minds are, in fact, changed when grace affects our lives. The idea of how all things are made new is a very welcomed reality of the Christian faith. "Do not be conformed to this world, but be transformed by the renewing of your minds" (Romans 12: 2).

There comes an understanding of God's gracious ways, God's plan for salvation through Jesus Christ, God's mercy, and God's divine love. There comes a new way of thinking, a new perspective. And we gain it all by grace. We gain it by growing in grace, by staying, abiding in Him. Remember, if anyone is in Christ ... Sanctifying grace can be known in spiritual growth. So think also about how we can grow spiritually. It comes through the practice of spiritual disciplines and through spiritual experience.

In 2 Corinthians, Paul spoke about the wisdom of Christ crucified, which is folly to the world:

We do, however, speak a message of wisdom among the mature, but not the wisdom of this Age or of the rulers of this age, who are coming to nothing. No, we declare God's wisdom, a Mystery that has been hidden and that God destined for our glory before time began. None of the rulers of this age understood it, for if they had, they would not have crucified the Lord of glory. However, as it is written:

> "What no eye has seen,
> what no ear has heard,
> and what no human mind has conceived-
> the things God has prepared for those who love him."

These are the things God has revealed to us by his Spirit. The Spirit searches all things, even the deep things of God. For who knows a person's thoughts except their own spirit within them? In the same way no one knows the thoughts of God except the Spirit of God. What we have received is not the spirit of the world, but the Spirit who is from God, so that we may understand what God has freely given us. This is what we speak, not in words taught us by human wisdom but in words taught by the Spirit, explaining spiritual realities with Spirit-taught words. The person without the Spirit does not accept the things that come from the Spirit of God but considers them foolishness, and cannot understand them because they are discerned only through the Spirit....

But we have the mind of Christ (2:6-16 NIV).

We have the mind of Christ. Thanks be to God. We can discern spiritual things. And we should think about these things.

Now it may seem as though I am sounding a bit redundant, and as someone from the Department of Redundancy Department, I apologize. But I can't stress enough the importance of the influence of our thoughts. In fact, Rene Descartes (1596-1650), the French philosopher and mathematician, was famous, in part, for his argument that deduced that "I think, therefore, I am." His wonderful conclusion, that we are thinking beings, is relevant in the context of this book. I believe, as did Descartes, that our thinking reveals not only that we exist, but that what we think can determine how we live. So we should think about these things.

It can make a difference.

Reflect, now, about where these chapters have taken you; I hope you will feel inspired to keep going in that direction. I may not be there yet, myself, but I am convinced (a thinking process) that I am gaining the heavenly mind as I consider the things that are true: trustworthy, reliable, real, constant, consistent, lasting, sound, valid, genuine, sincere, certain, legitimate, affirmative, faultless, perfect, unerring, honest.

Things that are honorable: noble, reputable, commendable, worthy, respectable, upstanding, scrupulous, steadfast, ethical, high-principled, and decent.

Things that are just: fair, right, righteous, equitable, legal, proper, correct, rational, and moral.

Things that are pure: uncorrupt, unadulterated, untainted, unsoiled, undefiled, innocent, guilt-free, and sinless, beyond reproach.

Things that are pleasing: lovely, delightful, beautiful, enjoyable, soothing, pleasant, agreeable, charming, appealing, adorable, splendid.

Things that are gracious: kind, benevolent, commendable, honorable, tender, considerate, nice, merciful, congenial, thoughtful, compassionate.

Things that are excellent: perfect, superb, valuable, meritorious, of good quality, above par, high caliber, virtuous, magnificent, wonderful, glorious, the best.

Things that are praiseworthy: laudable, worthy of compliment, pleasing, better than expected, blessed, admirable, well-deserving.

It is good to think about these things.

A Song

Look over your shoulder and see where you've been. And you'll know you can run, and you'll know you can win.

Because falling is harder than trying to rise, when you understand lows and you contemplate highs.

And the pain that is wisdom and the wound that's a cure cut through time as you notice you've learned to endure.

And the hope that brings sorrow and the joy that is grief and the dream that is truth area single belief.

But there's something ahead of you, something like truth, and the life that's behind you now calls itself youth.

And you know you can love, and you know you can bum, and you know that you're wiser; you know you can turn and be ready whenever your dreams come to because you can move mountains, and you can be free.

A Prayer

0 Lord, You have called on us to think in new and wonderful ways. Give us the strength we need to follow through. Give us the hope we need that will enable us to focus on what will help us seek the mind of Christ. And give us the sense of conviction we need to make the commitment to do so until we see things from the spiritual point of view. This we ask in the name of Jesus Christ, our Lord. Amen.

AND THEN ...

Do this in remembrance of Me.
- LU KE 22:1 9

With our minds, we remember. In churches, there is a practice of remembrance called Communion. In the Order of Communion, when the loaf has been broken and the cup has been lifted in the blessing of the elements, the officiating pastor then says, "Do this in remembrance of Me," quoting Jesus at His Last Supper. Part of the Liturgy, however, of the Great Thanksgiving remembers things that are specific about the life of Christ. Included in the general celebration of the Great Thanksgiving in the United Methodist Book of Worship, there follows particular memories of the life of Christ.

During the Season of Advent, what is remembered might also include words about the promise of a redeemer, of Christ's promised coming as Emmanuel, that He would be the light of the nations, and even about the hope of His promised Second Coming.

During the season of Christmastide, we might include words about the Incarnation, the Word made flesh, the humble setting of the stable, the annunciation of the angels, or even the greatest gift of all given by God in Jesus.

During the season of Epiphany, we might include words about the New Covenant, celebrating the purpose of the Incarnation as bringing the light to the nations, as acknowledged by the visit of the Wise Men (Magi), the Baptism of Jesus, the Transfiguration of Christ, and other images of His manifestation to the world.

During the season of Lent, we might remember, in particular, the forgiveness of Christ, His forty days of fasting and temptation, our delivery from slavery to sin and death.

There can also be a recollection of Christ's giving of Himself so humbly in His suffering, His sacrifice, His death, His Passion, His emptying of Himself, and His suffering servanthood.

During the season of Eastertide, of course we remember new life, the Resurrection, new birth, Christ's Ascension into heaven, and His promise to be with us always.

During the season of Pentecost, our words might also remember the way the Holy Spirit descended on Jesus at His Baptism, how the Spirit of the Lord was upon Him, how He gave the Holy Spirit, and how He gave birth to His Church, and how His Spirit continues to move in the hearts and lives of His disciples.

And during the long season called Ordinary Time, which I believe also should include Kingdomtide, from the end of August until Advent, we call to mind in the Great Thanksgiving many other aspects of the life of Christ, especially His teachings about the kingdom of God.

Sometimes, while people are quietly receiving the sacrament, and soft music is playing, a reader might offer passages of scripture such as the Beatitudes or the "I am ..." statements of Christ in the Gospel of John. Or songs relative to the Last Supper might be sung by the choir.

The point is that we can practice the remembrance of Christ. This aspect of worship should never be taken for granted. Even sermons can help us remember what we think about our Savior. But we remember. Communion is a sacrament of remembrance.

A sacrament can be defined as an outward and visible sign of an inward and spiritual grace. But everything we see, everything we hear, everything we can sense can be understood as a sign, a symbol of something more than itself. We can all be signs in this way. There is a deeper meaning that lay behind or through all things. And all things are able to point to some deeper meaning. The Bread of Communion is able to point us toward the Body of Christ. And the contents of the cup are able to point us toward the Blood of Christ. But what does it mean when we share these signs of God's grace? What does it mean when we eat the bread and drink from the cup? What is happening to us when we participate in this sacrament? What is happening within us when we don't?

Everything we do in life can be an outward and visible sign. It may not always be a sign of an inward and spiritual grace, but the way we live expresses our inner sense of values, our convictions, our priorities, our hopes, our fears, even our most inward thoughts. Sometimes, deep within, there might be something that is in the way of God's grace, or resistant to God's grace, or even a rejection of God's grace. Sometimes, within us, there is a wall.

Every act we do can tell the world what we believe in our hearts. If it's a competitive game, like baseball, perhaps the grace in our hearts helps us enjoy the re-creating pleasure of recreation. But if the pleasure is there only when we are winning, is it the grace of God who gave His Son that is moving within, or is it an ego need to be better than others?

"Do not be conformed to this world, but be transformed by the renewing of your minds, so that you may discern what the will of God is, what is good, and acceptable, and perfect" (Romans 12:2).

What's on your mind? What's in your heart? How do you express it? Do you express the will of God? Do you express the will of a believer? Do you express the hope and love of a Christian every day? Or do your outward acts express something unfaithful deep within you? Does your body, the outward sign, express your inner state of mind?

The body. "Just as the body without the spirit is dead, so faith without works is also dead" (James 2:26).

Our bodies express the fact of life within. But our bodies also express emotions, thoughts, attitudes. The Ninth Commandment tells us not to bear false witness. But perhaps the true witness is being born, for in spite of our hurts, we can still know God's love. In spite of our sadness and pain, we can still believe in God's comfort. In spite of the darkness all around us, we can still let our lights shine before others. But we must check ourselves (self-examination). Is what our bodies do really an outward and visible sign of an inward and spiritual grace? Or are we only able to bear witness to the light with some and not with others?

"The one who believes in Me will also do the works that I do"(John 14:12).

And then there are our words. Jesus said that "out of the abundance of the heart, the mouth speaks" (Luke 6:45). Much of what we say is an expression of what is within us. Sometimes, more often than our words, our tone of voice reveals our hearts, unless we are hypocrites (and of course, we all can be). "Little children, let us love, not [only] in word or speech, but in truth and action" (1 John 3:18).

In the Gospel of John, we are told that the Word became flesh. The Word of God is more than an expression of the mind of God! It is an outward and visible action. Jesus Christ is God's expression of spiritual grace. And the Bread and the Cup are Jesus's expression of spiritual Grace. If we take the Bread and Cup to heart, if we inwardly digest what it means to partake of the Body and Blood of Christ as we do in the celebration of Communion, then there is something that comes to our inward and spiritual self that, likewise, needs an outward and visible expression.

"The one who believes in Me will also do the works that I do and, in fact, will do greater things than these" (John 14:12).

Such is the power of remembrance, the power of the heavenly mind.

But we don't just remember. In Deuteronomy 6, where we have what is called the Great Commandment, and what is often referred to as the Shema (pronounced *shma*), because of the first word of the passage- Hear - we are told:

Hear, 0 Israel: The LORD our God, the LORD is one. Love the LORD your God with all your heart and with all your soul and with all your strength. These commandments that I give you today are to be on your hearts. Impress them on your children. Talk about them when you sit at home and when you walk along the road, when you lie down and when you get up.

Tie them as symbols on your hands and bind them on your foreheads. Write them on the doorframes of your houses and on your gates. (6:4-9 NIV)

I believe we are to talk about what we believe, about what God has done and is doing in our lives, and about what could happen in the lives of those who know us. We should especially talk about our love for God and God's love for us. When these things are manifested in our lives, others will know how wonderful faith can be. What we remember, what we believe, what we dream for our world, our hopes and desires: These are those wonderful intangibles that are so tangible in such amazing ways. And what we think can truly bless us.

Imagine archaeologists a thousand years from now discovering evidence of your life. What would they learn about you? What evidence would they find? What things would they witness? Would they be able to discern your thoughts? Would there be evidence that showed what you thought? One approach of crime scene investigators is to look at the evidence and try to figure out what the criminal was thinking. Likewise, an archaeologist will look at the evidence and try to discern the thoughts of those they are witnessing. If there were stories about you in the records of the local papers or recordings of the news, what would they say? We need to act in ways that are consistent with our beliefs and thoughts. That's integrity. Is your name on the rolls of a church? Is it included in the benevolence reports of any charity? Did you defend the helpless, did you feed the hungry, did you give water to the thirsty, did you welcome the stranger, clothe the naked, visit the sick or imprisoned? How will you be remembered? Will you have discerned ("proved,"

KJV) what is the will of God, what is good and excellent and perfect (Romans 12:2)?

Hopefully, you will be remembered, at least in part, for thinking these things and for having a heavenly mind.

One Last Story
A young man once journeyed from his home in the Land of Wisdom, not really knowing where he was going, what he would find, or who he would meet. And yet, he went out filled with hope and an eager mind. In some respects, he knew that his destination was his starting point, for he believed he would one day return. The only difference was, he knew, that nothing would be the same, because he would never be the same. And so he understood that the real purpose of his journey was change. His only expectation, however, was that he might learn something new. He believed that if he expected from others more than they could offer, then he was wrapped up in his own expectations and unable to receive what others might be able to give to him. So he actually didn't expect anything in particular but was willing to accept whatever gifts might come.

All his life, growing up in the Land of Wisdom, he had learned that wisdom could never fill his heart. It only made him hungrier. His true search, he discovered, was for the purpose of wisdom. And he felt that the purpose was always going to be just beyond whatever he thought it was, for he knew that the furthest anyone can ever really see was to the beginning of their own blindness, and the most anyone can ever know reaches only to the border of their own ignorance. Even though he was from the Land of Wisdom, he knew wisdom was not something he could ever possess, the same way that someone who comes from the sunlight into the darkness cannot bring the light with them.

It was not that he was filled with doubt, for all doubt is actually self-doubt. Doubt exists only in the mind of one who either cannot believe or who simply cannot accept the truth. And though he was not about to sit back and just believe anything he was told, he began his journey with an open mind, convinced that there are probably no new truths, only newly conceived points of view. Soon, however, he learned that this was only half-right. And he discovered that it is better to be all-right half the time than to be half-right all the time.

And it was not that he was filled with fear. Fear is more like the pain that's felt when a wound is anticipated. He had no fear (maybe he was a little naive), only wonder and curiosity. And there was a hunger. But his hunger was there, not because of an emptiness, but because of a desire for more truth. And one of the first things he learned as he began his journey was that the only way a person can breathe in a new breath is after they've released a breath. In order to become more, he had to be willing to become less. In order to receive, he would have to let go. And this he learned over and over again, until he came to understand the truth that in order to be something, to be anything at all, a person had to be willing to become nothing. This he learned from a Christian.

The Christian told him many things about God, the source of all truth, the Creator of all things, who is all-knowing, all-powerful, and ever-present. He learned that wisdom was only one of God's many attributes, one that seemed even less relevant than God's mercy or love or compassion or grace. Wisdom was always in the background, though, an ever-pervasive Holy Spirit. As such, it is part of all that God is. Still, God is beyond the grasp of human wisdom or understanding. God is known by something called faith. The human mind can be filled with the knowledge of God, but that knowledge can only be partial in this life. The vessel of the human mind overflows, for it cannot contain all there is to know about God. Human nature is fallen, and it seems to cherish, almost boast of the human ability to understand and reason, almost to the point of worship, as if wisdom was God. But God is wisdom, and God is more. To worship a single attribute of God is to fall far short of the truth. "Be not wise in your own eyes," the Christian said. Learn words from God's teaching, for human understanding is folly to God. Whereas even the foolishness of God is wiser than human wisdom. Therefore, said the teachings, let the one who boasts boast in God, for God has made foolish the wisdom of the world.

So we are fools when we apply our worldly wisdom to life and not the wisdom of God. We are fools even when we judge others to be fools, for it is what we don't like in ourselves that we cannot tolerate in others; when we find fault in others, we are really finding fault in ourselves. We do not make our own lights shine any brighter by diminishing the radiance of another. Such is the folly of human wisdom. What we must learn is the way of the cross. And the word of the cross is folly to those who are perishing.

In his quest, the young man from the Lan d of Wisdom sought to understand nothing but the wisdom of the cross. He learned that, all too often, people pay far too much attention to who they are (or, actually, who they think they are), and to what they have been, and to what they think they are becoming, when others need those people to pay attention to them, to what they are becoming and how they can help them. You see, the young man learned that God revealed Himself completely in Jesus Christ, who died on the cross, who did not pay attention to Himself, although He could have. He did not count equality with God a thing to be held onto. He emptied Himself. He took on the form of a servant. He looked not to His own interests, but to the needs of others, dying for their sins, dying on the cross for the sins of the whole world, becoming a sacrifice so that others might live. Jesus showed love so that the world might learn how to love others, even their enemies.

The young man's journey had ended. He returned to his home. He was a changed man. He learned that the purpose of wisdom is not understanding, but faith, and that the wisdom of faith is the foolishness of the cross. And he felt called to tell others in his homeland about love, not in lofty words or wisdom, but simply by sharing nothing but Jesus Christ and Him Crucified: the way of the cross.

And he changed the name of the land. Now the Land of Wisdom is called the Land of Innocence. It is the land where many go to begin their journeys, but where all too few can find a home. They cannot stay there because they do not belong, save for starting their journeys.

And if the journey seems to have no end, it is because this journey is our destination.

What to Do

Read it all again.

A Prayer

0 God, You are working in me to complete me. Help me let You do Your job. Help me let You finish me. I cannot do it myself. I know You are not done with me. I know You may have a long way to go. And I know You are going with me. Thank You for never giving up on me. And thank You for giving me the ideas of what I can think about. Please, give me a heavenly mind. I ask this in Jesus's name. Amen.

One Last Word
and then I'm done

> Keep on doing the things that you have learned
> and received and heard and seen in me,
> and the God of peace will be with you.
> PHILIPPIANS 4:9

One verse before Paul tells the Philippians, "Finally..., think about these things," he spoke about a particular result of prayer, telling them that "the peace of God, which surpasses all understanding, will guard your hearts and your minds in Christ Jesus" (verse 7). Then we receive the list of things to think about. The list is sandwiched between two commendations of peace. Think... do it... and "the God of peace will be with you" (verse 9)

Peace. Peace of mind. It is so glorious that it is beyond our human understanding! It is not just an absence of conflict, but the presence of serenity, of assurance, of reconciliation, of wholeness. Jesus is the Prince of Peace. His presence can give that sense of how everything is all right. We need this experience. We want peace. We seek it, and we cherish those brief moments when we know peace is upon us. Peace is a gift. It is often taken for granted. But peace is also a consequence. Paul says that what we have learned, what we have received, what we have heard, and what we have seen in him, we should do. As we practice what we understand; as we celebrate what we have been given; as we absorb what we listen to; and as we follow the example of our teacher, we will experience some of the ways the peace of God will be with us.

I truly believe that thinking about whatever is true, honorable, just, pure, pleasing, gracious, excellent, and worthy of praise will help to bring us peace.

The best last word is just that:

> Peace.
> In faith, with hope, out of love,
> Tom

www.ingramcontent.com/pod-product-compliance
Lightning Source LLC
LaVergne TN
LVHW040146080526
838202LV00042B/3039